To John
With my v[illegible] [illegible]shes,
Chisanga
June 29, 2015

GETTING ZAMBIA TO WORK

Published by
Adonis & Abbey Publishers Ltd
P.O. Box 43418
London
SE11 4XZ
http://www.adonis-abbey.com
Email: editor@adonis-abbey.com

First Edition, September 2011

British Library Cataloguing-in-Publication Data
A catalogue record for this book is available from the British Library

ISBN: 9781906704872 (HB)/ 9781906704865 (PB)

Printed and bound in Great Britain

GETTING ZAMBIA TO WORK

BY

Chisanga Puta-Chekwe

PREFACE

Writing a current affairs book about any young country is a challenge because of the rapid pace at which events unfold and change. Writing about Zambia is no exception. Still, over the past fifty years that Zambia has been independent some practices have become entrenched and come close to being traditions. These practices have influenced Zambian socio economic development. More often than not that influence has been negative.

The question often asked about Zambia is, why has the country not achieved even a fraction of its potential? A friend working for the World Bank in Lusaka asked me pointedly one day why Zambia "with such an intelligent population" had to depend on foreign aid. The answer to that question lies, at least in part, in post independence Zambian culture. I have therefore attempted to demonstrate how the post independence Zambian culture has hindered development.

But this book is not just about culture and its impact on Zambian economic development. It is also about specific decisions that were made and also about the impact of the very character of some of the main players on the political scene. This book seeks to identify some of the historic decisions that contributed to Zambia's plight and failure to realise her potential. But the book is also a commentary on today's economic and political reality. I hope the reader will find that both the past and the present have been used appropriately to suggest the way forward for this potentially rich land.

In addition to reading relevant books on Zambia, I have used the internet extensively for research. Much of what I found on the internet proved inadequate and unproven. In those circumstances, I either did not use the material or sought confirmation of the material elsewhere. Perhaps most importantly I have conducted many conversations with people in Zambia and elsewhere.

Most of these people offered a credible perspective and potential solutions. The least productive discussions were those I had with persons currently connected to the Zambian government. But even here there were exceptions. These tended to be senior public servants appointed to their positions on merit rather than through political patronage.

Though I hesitate to single out individuals for special mention I should like particularly to thank my great friend Martin Lumb for his encouragement, his willingness to go over the manuscript, and for helping me find a suitable publisher. When I was just beginning the task of writing I asked another friend Caroline Linehan to read the first two chapters and comment on the accessibility of my writing to ordinary intelligent readers. She took on this task happily and executed the exercise expeditiously

A huge amount of Zambian history remains unwritten and for this reason it is often necessary to seek reliable oral sources to fill the gap. Both my mother Grace and my aunt Flavia Musonda Musakanya provided useful insight on the reality of living under a regime not instinctively respectful of human rights. At different times in the past, each was obliged to run the family business in the absence of an imprisoned husband. Both experienced alienation as well as solidarity and learnt a great deal about practical politics. I thank them for their willingness to pass on their knowledge.

For useful information about the development of law in modern Zambia and the intersection between law and politics, I turned to my uncle Bruce Munyama. I thank him for spending hours with me explaining some of the landmark cases that came to influence the way corruption is perceived and dealt with in the country. As a respected lawyer, he also gave me a unique view of the development of Zambia's legal institutions.

Mr. Greene Simpungwe was kind enough to talk to me about his experiences in both the public and private sectors of Zambia. His knowledge of the history of nationalisation is most impressive. I thank him and Dr. Silane Mwenechanya who also talked to me at length about the mining sector and, more generally, possible ways of increasing individual wealth in Zambia.

Over the years many friends have suggested that I write a book on Zambia. I thank all of them for their encouragement. Let me be clear however that while I have learnt a great deal from these friends and other people I have consulted, I am solely responsible for the content of this book.

I also thank my wife Jean for her understanding as I took over the dining room table which I found more conducive to writing than the desk in the study.

Chisanga Puta-Chekwe
Burlington, Ontario
December 2010

DEDICATION

This book is dedicated to the memory of:

- Denis Katongo Baines, mechanic, community leader, entrepreneur, businessman, political prisoner
- Dingiswayo Hayden Banda, community organiser, campaigner for independence, cabinet minister, leader of the opposition.
- Pete Paul Banda, early university graduate, teacher, linguist, nationalist
- Sir Stewart Gore Brown, legislator, nationalist, adventurist
- Linda Burton, housewife and victim of political murder.
- Tolomeo Bwalya, musician, nationalist
- Musonda Chambeshi, trade unionist, politician, businessman, community leader, political prisoner
- Alick Chanda, patriot, snake expert, biologist
- Jameson Chapoloko, trade unionist, politician, deputy speaker of the national assembly, political prisoner.
- Patrick Chella, alumnus of Lubwa Mission School, nationalist, educationist, national honouree
- Julia Chikamoneka (Mama UNIP) nationalist, community organiser, women's leader, tireless campaigner for Zambian independence
- Martha Chileshe, women's leader, commissioner of the Girl Guide movement
- Safeli Chileshe, pioneer, civic leader, first indigenous mayor of Lusaka, first indigenous director of Roan Selection Trust mining company, businessman, adjudicator.
- Chilimboyi, Member of the African Representative Council (MARC)
- Anna Chilombo, teacher, saleswoman, fish trader, first woman to own a shop in Fort Rosebery (Mansa), Kabwe based businesswoman, political prisoner
- Bentley Chima, trade unionist, community leader
- Justin Musonda Chimba, community leader, trade unionist, campaigner for independence, politician, pioneer cabinet minister, opposition leader, political prisoner
- Patrick Chisanga, public servant, political prisoner
- John Chisata, trade unionist, politician, political prisoner, businessman.

- Joseph Mutale Chisengalumbwe, first indigenous Regimental Sergeant Major (RSM), in the Northern Rhodesia Kings African Rifles, community leader, pioneer
- Godfrey "Ucar" Chitalu, footballer, coach of the national soccer team
- Frank Chitambala, community leader, trade unionist, politician
- Harry Chiyungi, trade unionist
- Mainza Chona, nationalist, first indigenous lawyer, politician, attorney general, prime minister, legal practitioner
- John (Jack) Dare Q.C., O.B.E, legal representative of the Northern Rhodesia African Mineworkers' Union, civic leader, Ndola City Council alderman, legal practitioner, high court commissioner
- Jimmy Fleming, advocate for racial justice, supporter of Northern Rhodesia African Mineworkers Union, businessman, football administrator
- Professor Lameck Kazembe Hazal Goma, alumnus of Lubwa Mission School in Chinsali, renowned biologist, lecturer in Zoology at Makerere University, in Uganda and University of Ghana, Legon (Accra), the first indigenous vice-chancellor of the University of Zambia.
- Richard Hall, author, historian, journalist, editor in chief of the Times of Zambia
- Barbara Hall, author of popular agony aunt column 'Tell me Josephine'
- John Hunt, nationalist, campaigner for democracy, victim of political harassment
- HE Habanyama, politician, MARC
- Roger Henderson, batsman, captain of Zambian Cricket team
- M Kakumbi, legislator
- Hank Kalanga, trade unionist, politician.
- The Kalela dancers of the Copperbelt who campaigned for independence through song and dance
- Reuben Chitandika Kamanga, first vice president of the Republic of Zambia
- Lucy Chisha Kanondo, first indigenous nurse
- Anne Kapotwe, women's leader, teacher, community worker
- Ediwn Sunny Kapotwe M.B.E., civil servant, diplomat, business executive

- Simon Mwansa Kapwepwe, alumnus of Lubwa Mission School, journalist, linguist, community leader, founding member of the Northern Rhodesia African National Congress, founding member of the Zambia African National Congress, founding member of United National Independence Party, first foreign minister of Zambia, vice president of Zambia, founder of the United Progressive Party, political prisoner.
- Chola Lawrence Katilungu, trade unionist, politician, MARC
- Gwen Konie, first indigenous female graduate, public servant, diplomat, politician.
- Godwin Mbikusita Lewanika, federal Member of Parliament, trade unionist, politician
- Bob Litana, preacher, teacher, farmer
- W.C. Little, Munali School headmaster, educationist
- Berrings Lombe, ANC Katanga representative, ANC deputy national secretary, ardent supporter of a coalition government between ANC and UNIP after the inconclusive elections of 1962.
- Naxon Longwe, early graduate, civic leader, mayor of Chingola, businessman
- Henry Makulu, early supporter of African National Congress, nationalist, educator, promoter of youth interest
- Monica Makulu, community leader, teacher
- Michael Mataka, first indigenous police commissioner of Zambia Police
- Job Michello, trade unionist, ally of Katilungu, replaced Katilungu in Legislative assembly after latter's death, politician
- Agness Morton, beloved broadcaster
- Stephen Mpashi, Bemba language author
- Elijah Mudenda, author, scientist, nationalist, prime minister
- Titus Mukupo, nationalist leader, politician, journalist, editor of *Zambia News*, Chief Information Officer
- Humphrey Mulemba, campaigner for independence, politician, UNIP cabinet minister, UNIP Secretary General and Vice President of the republic, high commissioner to Canada, MMD cabinet minister, opposition politician, businessman
- Yotam Muleya, athlete of international repute

- Nalumino Mundia, campaigner for independence, cabinet minister, founder of the United Party, political prisoner, prime minister, ambassador to the United States
- Valentine Shula Musakanya, thinker, inventor, first secretary of cabinet, pilot, founder of the flying school in Zambia, governor of the central bank, businessman, political prisoner.
- G. Musumbulwa, civic leader, politician MARC
- John Mupanga Mwanakatwe, first indigenous university graduate, teacher, first indigenous principal of a high school, public servant, politician, education minister, finance minister, lawyer, chancellor of the university of Zambia, and author.
- Patrick Mwanawasa, businessman, community leader, treasurer of the Northern Rhodesia Traders' Association.
- Levy Patrick Mwanawasa, human rights lawyer, president for the republic of Zambia.
- Bestin Mwanza, guitarist, pianist, nationalist.
- Petros Mwenechanya, community leader and trade unionist
- Robinson Nabulyato, legislator, speaker of the National Assembly
- Princess Nakatindi, daughter of Paramount Chief Yeta III of Barotseland, Member of the Mongu-Lealui District Education Authority, Director of the UNIP Women's' Brigade, Member of Parliament, District Governor of Sesheke, Member of the House of Chiefs, mother of 11 children
- Mashekwa Nalumango, nationalist, medical doctor, politician, public servant, dairy farmer.
- Samuel "Zoom" Ndhlovu, footballer, national football team skipper.
- Lakement Ng'andu (later Mutale Chitapankwa), civic leader, administrator, politician, legislator, MARC, businessman, paramount Chief of the Bemba
- Kenan Ng'ambi, Commissioner of the Boy Scout movement
- Alick Nkhata, musician, broadcaster, nationalist, farmer
- Mukuka Nkoloso, nationalist, Latin scholar, campaigner for independence, space travel enthusiast, victim of political torture
- Brian Nkonde, broadcaster, educationist, businessman, first indigenous mayor of Broken Hill (Kabwe), politician, farmer

- Harry Mwaanga Nkumbula, community leader, teacher, president of the African National Congress, political prisoner, pre independence minister of African education, businessman
- Professor Nkunika, chemist, educationist.
- Vincent Nsomi, scientist, teacher, business executive
- R.D. Patel, supporter of Zambian independence, trader and founder of Kanjombe Stores
- Marta Paynter, journalist (first journalist to arrive at scene of crash where Secretary General Hammarskjöld died), proud Zambian by choice.
- Wesley Pillsbury Nyirenda, alumnus of Lubwa Mission School, early graduate, secondary school principal, speaker of the national assembly.
- Robinson Chisanga Puta, alumnus of Lubwa Mission School, trade unionist, businessman, founding Chairman and CEO of Zambia Railways Board, politician, MARC, Officer of the Commanding Order of Freedom (O.C.F.), founding member of the United Progressive Party, political prisoner
- John Mukuka Puta, business manager, civic leader, businessman, commercial farmer
- Bwalya Pat Puta, local government administrator, football administrator, broadcaster, businessman, supporter of indigenous talent
- Edward Jack Shamwana, lawyer, chairman of the Law Association of Zambia, political prisoner
- Joseph Shaw, accountant, campaigner for Zambian independence, Secretary of Bancroft Chamber of Commerce, director of Bank of Zambia, businessman
- Mable Shaw, devoted teacher of young women at Mbereshi Girls Boarding School
- Whittington Sikalumbi, nationalist, politician
- Akwila Simpasa, fine artist, sculptor, musician,
- James Simukonda, veterinarian, community leader, and businessman
- Donald Siwale, civil servant, national honouree, nationalist, MARC.
- James Skinner, first Zambian minister of justice, recipient of the Grand Commander by Order of Menelik II of Ethiopia, Attorney-General, mediator in a dispute between Kenya and

Somalia which resulted in the Arusha settlement, through which the two countries reopened diplomatic relations, Chief Justice of Zambia.

- Hamish Cameron Smith, proud Zambian, former prisoner of war, architect
- Malama Sokoni, alumnus of Lubwa Mission School, nationalist, politician, MARC
- Pascale Sokota, civic leader, legislator, MARC, businessman
- Henry Tayali, abstract painter and artist of international repute
- Gershom Temba, alumnus of Lubwa Mission School, District Assistant in the colonial civil service in the late 1950s, supporter of Zambian independence, first indigenous District Commissioner of Mazabuka and Kabwe, campaigner for democracy in post independence Zambia
- Edwin Sushi Wabo, business executive, political prisoner.
- Arthur Wina, intellectual, politician, first Zambian finance minister, first chairman of the Movement for Multiparty Democracy.
- Dauti Yamba, civic leader, politician, legislator, MARC
- David Yumba, broadcaster, host of longest running radio talk show, *Kabusha takolelwe bowa.*

TABLE OF CONTENTS

INTRODUCTION

The tragedy of the last one hundred years is that Zambians have been deluded into believing, contrary to all common sense and history, that they are not capable of running their own country successfully, without either foreign help or a paternalistic government. This book seeks to show that this notion is not only ludicrous and injurious, but also misplaced. The book suggests practical and often simple ways in which Zambia can lift herself out of the current malaise and become a world class economy and master of her own destiny.

The lack of national self confidence resulting from the delusion of incapacity has led to national decline and an unhealthy dependency on what is seen as foreign largesse. That largesse of course comes at a price, increasing Zambia's dependency, and making it harder for the country to control its destiny, fight poverty and prosper.

But the decline has not been merely economic; it has also been moral and political. In the post independence era, the culture of mutual support, so evident in traditional Zambian society, has all but disappeared, giving way instead to a culture of neglect and avarice. Zambia's political structures, designed for the purpose of advancing individual political agendas, have generally failed to facilitate genuine democratic expression for the people as a whole. It is no wonder that the country now has virtually no credible public institutions and certainly no independent or professional civil service.

The decline of the nation has inevitably led to polarised and overly partisan politics so that 'solutions' provided by political institutions are necessarily partisan and fleeting.

Much has been made of the fact that Zambia's economic growth rate of six per cent toward the end of the first decade of this century is extraordinary and evidence that extreme poverty may yet be eliminated. The fact however is, six per cent growth is miniscule for a country starting from Zambia's low economic base. More importantly this rate of economic growth does not reflect the country's true potential.

The country would have to at least double its current growth rate in order to have a more realistic chance of alleviating poverty and setting the nation on the path of self-reliance and sustainable prosperity.

To stop Zambia's economic decline, the country must also halt its political degeneration. Creating a truly independent electoral commission, separating more rigorously the powers of the legislature, the executive, and the judiciary, will make Zambian democracy more robust and provide a mechanism for building a new consensus.

Lasting wealth is created by free and innovative people governed by regimes with unquestionable commitment to the welfare of their people. The free market system must be made to work primarily for the benefit of the Zambian without discrimination as to creed, place of birth, mother tongue, colour, or country of origin. Thus the purpose of industrial regeneration must be to maximise employment opportunities for nationals. Needless to say, investment in the education of nationals must be a priority and its purpose must be to equip the Zambian workforce with the capacity to function successfully and effectively in the technological environment of the 21st century. Other developmental priorities must include health and food security.

The people of Zambia have what it takes to create a great nation. They need not defer to anyone in matters affecting the development of their country. They are quite capable of running their affairs successfully; and now is the time for Zambians to take charge and be responsible for their destiny.

CHAPTER 1

Fall from Grace

When Whittington Sikalumbi suggested that Northern Rhodesia be renamed Zambezia at the end of British colonial rule, he was supported by Simon Mwansa Kapwepwe whose only proviso was that the new name should be truncated to the more euphonious Zambia. It is probable however that euphony was less important than the values that the ancient state of Zambezia represented. The country's Zambezian ancestors had an unwritten constitution that obliged their 'king of kings' to govern fairly. The king's authority rested on election, and he could be deposed in the event of abuse of authority or failure to use power wisely. There can be little doubt that had Zambezia continued to exist in its original form, it would have developed an impressive political dispensation that guaranteed political diversity. This conclusion flows from the fact that in the 10th century Zambezia, a premium was already placed on good governance.

It is a matter of regret that commitment to good governance in modern Zambia diminished significantly within a few years of attaining independence, and was finally dealt a near fatal blow (which placed democracy in a comatose state for almost two decades) with the introduction of the one party system of government in 1972. Ironically, one of the arguments advanced in favour of the one party system of government, whose effect was to reduce political justice and equity, was that this system was more in keeping with 'traditional African systems of government'. The argument was patently false and is certainly contradicted by the Zambezia experience. Despite the obvious intellectual dishonesty of this argument, it was not unusual to find otherwise respectable people echoing the official line that Zambia's one party state was democratic.

This dishonesty was to lead to the curtailment of critical thought and an almost total erasure of any memory suggesting that democratic development and good governance were compatible with traditional Zambian values. To demonstrate the relevance of democracy and good governance one did not in fact have to go as far back as Zambezia.

The nationalists who campaigned heroically against colonial rule relied on the limited democratic space offered by the colonial administration to mobilise public opinion against continued British rule. Indeed, the United National Independence Party (UNIP), the largest nationalist movement toward the end of colonial rule, issued a declaration of human rights in 1958 that included the unambiguous right to form and belong to political parties. The sudden realisation then that pluralism was not compatible with traditional African systems of government must have come a few years after the nationalist movement attained power. UNIP had of course won the 1964 election democratically. Sadly there was only one other democratic election after that, until the peaceful return to democracy in 1991.

In democratic Zambia, numerous hours are spent by leaders attending seminars on good governance, a topic that has also provided ample opportunity for foreign travel. While the seriousness with which the subject of good governance is taken, is welcome, it also serves as a reminder of how much Zambia has regressed. Zambians are learning about good governance in the 21st century, when their ancestors had developed the concept in the 10th century!

Governance in Modern Zambia

The Constitution negotiated between the nationalists and the departing colonial authority paid little attention to governance in traditional Southern African society. Indeed the belief of many involved in the negotiations was that traditional Zambia had nothing to offer in this regard. Consequently, the Zambian Constitution of 1964 did not consciously reflect the Zambezian values referred to above or even the values of a later state, the Kingdom of Kongo, ancestral origin of the majority of modern Zambia's population.

The Kingdom of Kongo was founded in the thirteenth century. It was ruled by a monarch known as the *ManiKongo*. As with the king of Zambezia, the *ManiKongo* was elected by an assembly of clan leaders. He dispensed justice from his capital at Mbaza Kongo, although according to oral history he avoided involvement in minor legal issues affecting the daily lives of his citizens. Thus he concerned himself only with legal issues of import usually affecting relations with foreign powers or treasonous subjects. Legal matters such as alleged adultery would be dealt with by a first judge known as a *mani vangu vangu*. This was but one of a number of specialised positions in the *ManiKongo's* sophisticated civil service. The kingdom was divided into six provinces, each led by a governor appointed by the king.

Although there appears no evidence to suggest that the king had a constitutional obligation to govern all the people with equity, as in the case of Zambezia's 'king of kings', it is beyond question that the *ManiKongo* could only rule successfully through an elaborate and constitutional requirement to consult the representatives of free citizens widely.

It is a matter of regret that no modern Zambian constitution has created institutions that (by design) genuinely obliged the executive branch (the presidency) to consult the people's representatives.

Instead, all Zambian constitutions to date have been based on a fusion of the American and British models of governance. Fusing these two systems of government has not worked well for the country and has in fact undermined democracy, and on one occasion eradicated it completely.

The post independence constitutional dispensation has provided for a president as head of state. There has also been a vice president chosen either by the president or the ruling party but not by the population at large. The position of vice president was abolished during the one party era and the responsibilities of the office shared between the Party Secretary General and the Prime Minister. In the hierarchy of the day the Party Secretary General took precedence over the Prime Minister, who sat in the legislature and acted as leader of the national assembly. The positions of Secretary General and Prime Minister were abolished when the country returned to democracy, and the office of Vice President was revived.

Zambia's vice president, unlike his US counterpart, has been more than a passive member of the legislature. He has a substantive role as Leader of the House, controlling the legislative agenda. The Vice President's position is undoubtedly fortified by the fact that all his cabinet colleagues are required to sit in parliament.

Unelected politicians wanting to serve as cabinet ministers may be nominated to the legislature and enjoy all the rights and privileges of elected members of the House. At the time of writing the president may nominate up to eight unelected members of the legislature.

Thus far no constitution has provided for a limit on the number of members of the Executive who may sit in Parliament.

This flaw in the constitution has been exploited by presidents, at the expense of democratic development. It has not taken long for them to realise that the legislature can be controlled simply by increasing the number of executive members sitting in parliament. A large executive presence in parliament coupled with rigorous enforcement of the principle of collective responsibility, has in practice helped the president to pass without difficulty any legislation desired.

At the time of writing there are 150 elected members of parliament and eight nominated legislators. Out of that total figure of 158, 66 are government ministers and therefore members of the executive branch of government. Of the remaining 92 members, many aspire to be cabinet ministers (regardless of political affiliation) and will therefore be careful not to be too critical of the government.

Even if these members were all prepared to be critical of government however, it would be impossible for them to force an amendment to the constitution, which requires an affirmative vote by 106 parliamentarians, or two thirds of the legislators. Under the principle of collective responsibility, the 66 parliamentarians who serve in the executive branch must support the government. Furthermore it is the responsibility of the chief whip to ensure that even those parliamentarians (from the ruling party) who are not members of the Government always vote with the Executive.

Parliament has thus been denied the opportunity to be truly independent and to effectively represent the constituents across the country. The shortcomings of the Zambian constitution in this regard are now recognised, as evidenced by submissions made to the National Constitutional Conference.

The Road to Dictatorship

The year 1964 was a watershed in Zambia's political development. After painstaking negotiations, a new constitution for the country was agreed between the new nationalist-dominated government and the departing colonial administration. For the first time in the history of Zambia the qualifications for voters as set out in the Electoral Provisions (Qualifications of Voters) Regulations, were based on the principle of universal franchise, with the minimum voting age set at 21 years.

The right to vote was not confined to Zambian citizens, as British subjects and other non Zambians who met certain residence qualifications were eligible to participate, and many did. The racial history of the territory was reflected in the 'roll' system which provided for 65 main roll and 10 reserved roll constituencies. Black Zambians, or 'Africans', as they were known, were registered as main roll voters and 'Europeans' as reserved roll voters. These classifications of course simplified the racial divide of the country and left many dissatisfied as to their ethnic or racial identity. The authorities addressed this simplistic classification by allowing those who were neither Africans nor Europeans to choose the roll they wished to be registered on. Not an insignificant number of mixed race people chose to be classified as European, while some ethnic Indians, like Kanoobhai Patel, who subsequently became a councillor on the Mufulira Municipal Council, were content to be classified as Africans.

Altogether, one million three hundred and eighty people registered as voters, representing ninety-two per cent of eligible voters. At this time the president of the country was not elected directly, being chosen instead by the National Assembly candidates who indicated the presidential candidate of their choice. The votes received by these candidates were simultaneously given to their choice for president.

The United National Independence Party won 56 seats while the African National Congress, which had ruled with UNIP in the pre-independence coalition government since 1962, took nine seats. UNIP's leader, Kenneth Kaunda, became the first president of the Republic of Zambia on October 24, 1964 upon the country attaining independence.

Few would have believed that this triumph of democracy over colonial rule, which had distinguished itself for its failure to hold a single democratic election, would be short-lived. But within a decade of the 1964 election, Zambia was placed firmly on the road to dictatorship.

The election of December 10, 1968, had 105 National Assembly seats at stake. UNIP won 81 while ANC took 23, with the remaining seat going to an independent candidate. Despite the ANC increasing its representation of seats in the National Assembly, plans were already underway to turn Zambia into a one party state. The stated hope was that the one party state would come about 'democratically', with the ANC being decimated at future polls.

It is doubtful however that this commitment to end formal opposition through the ballot box was honestly held. Despite the Opposition increasing its share of seats in the 1968 election (from 12 per cent to 21 per cent), UNIP continued to be disrespectful of the office of leader of the opposition, if not to the very idea of parliamentary democracy. The UNIP leader was on record as saying that it would 'pay to belong to UNIP'. That soon became a mantra and justified the employment of only UNIP loyalists in public institutions. Steps were also taken to withdraw formal recognition of the leader of the opposition, and to evict him from his official residence. In doing so, the ruling party purported to rely on guidelines provided by the famed constitutional law expert Erskine May who suggested a minimum number of seats that would entitle an opposition party to claim the status of official opposition. There is however nothing in established constitutional law and parliamentary practice that prevents a government from according official status to a party that falls short of the magic number. Indeed the practice in modern democracies is to recognise "the member who heads the largest party elected to Parliament that is not the governing party", as Leader of the Opposition. The quote is from the official website of the Western Cape Provincial Parliament. The South African jurisdiction considers "an effective Opposition essential for a democracy to function properly."

There is an even better example from Ontario. After the 1999 election support for the opposition New Democratic Party fell significantly leaving the party with just eight seats.

Under the rules of the Legislative Assembly, a party could only receive official status, and the resources and privileges accorded to officially-recognized parties, if it had 12 or more members in the House. The NDP did not have the requisite number of members. It now had only eight bodies. The governing Progressive Conservative Party however changed the rules after the election to lower the threshold for party status from 12 seats to eight. This action was more consistent with the democratic norms than UNIP's haste to strip the ANC of official status.

More ominously, UNIP showed itself adept at political expediency, and indifferent to human rights. The 1964 Constitution had entrenched clauses protecting fundamental human rights. These clauses could only be amended by a two- thirds majority in parliament as well as the approval of the electorate in a referendum.

The UNIP Government held a referendum in 1969 seeking approval for the amendment of the constitution so that in future parliament could amend entrenched clauses with a two thirds majority without resort to referenda.

The debate preceding the referendum was dominated by the UNIP government which argued that the constitutional change was the only way to make land privately held by absentee landlords available for use by Zambians. At a time when there was plenty of land for those wishing to engage in farming, it was never explained why the matter of land confiscation had become so urgent. In the circumstances, sceptics who feared that the exercise had more to do with the consolidation of power than fair distribution of land had much to support their case. Harry Mwaanga Nkumbula, the leader of the opposition, was one such sceptic. He warned that amending the constitution in this way would only pave the way for dictatorship and would do nothing to help the poor people of Zambia. But in the days following independence few were prepared to listen to a politician they considered 'soft' on colonial rule. To many, taking over the 'land owned by foreigners' was a natural part of the process of liberating the country from the colonial yoke. Nkumbula's warnings that the amendment would undermine human rights thus fell on deaf ears.

A "yes" vote would have been a defeat for the UNIP Government as it would have led to retention of the referendum requirement, while a "no" vote authorised the removal of the requirement. When the votes were tallied, the "yes" side had 15 per cent, while the "no" side had 85 per cent. UNIP had scored a huge victory.

One Party State

The 1969 referendum was to be the last free vote for Zambians for more than two decades. With the entrenched provisions of the constitution removed, the UNIP government was under no legal obligation, although perhaps they had a moral one, to hold a special election or referendum to authorise the introduction of the one party state.

When the charismatic former vice president, Simon Mwansa Kapwepwe and a number of leading politicians broke away from UNIP to formal a rival opposition party known as the United Progressive

Party, Kenneth Kaunda moved quickly to both deal with the new party and hasten the process of converting Zambia into a one party state. UPP, formed on August 22nd 1971, posed the first real threat to UNIP. It captured the imagination of the politically crucial Copperbelt Province and even won the support of some intellectuals, notably at the University of Zambia.

It is fair to say that Kaunda's reaction to the UPP was influenced more by fear than rational analysis. The majority of support for the new party came from the Bemba speaking areas of the country. Since these areas have a reputation for political independence and objectivity, it is unlikely that they would have instinctively and unquestioningly continued to support Mr. Kapwepwe and thereby given him the mandate he sought to remove Kaunda as president of the country. Furthermore, the intelligentsia had elements in the early 1970s that were suspicious of Simon Kapwepwe whom they saw as a hard line traditionalist. The support of intellectuals at the University of Zambia, notwithstanding, Kapwepwe would not have been able to count on unqualified support from the Bemba intelligentsia indefinitely. In addition, the Zambian economy had not yet completely collapsed and the warnings issued by Kapwepwe about what he saw as the coming economic catastrophe and corruption, seemed remote to many people.

All these factors, combined with the power of incumbency which favoured Kaunda and his party, would almost certainly have resulted in Kaunda defeating Kapwepwe at the next election. But even that was not acceptable to Kaunda who increasingly saw himself as life president of a one party state. Kaunda could not take the risk of allowing Kapwepwe a formal position on the political stage, outside the ruling party. Certainly an effective leader of the opposition would make it more difficult to convert Zambia into a one party state.

The even greater danger from Kaunda's point of view was that, in time, Kapwepwe might persuade enough people to support him in his bid to remove UNIP (and therefore Kaunda) from power.

Within days of the formation of UPP in 1971, Kaunda imprisoned three leaders of the new party, including Ray Banda and Zilole Mumba, the most prominent and visible leaders from the Eastern Province. This move left at large only leaders from the Copperbelt, Luapula, Northern, and Central Provinces. All these leaders were seen as Bemba speaking, and thus, at a stroke, Kenneth Kaunda was able to brand the new party as an ethnic rather than a national organisation. Credence was given to this claim when respected non Bemba leaders like Elijah Mudenda, who subsequently became Prime Minister in the Second Republic, defied expectation and failed to join the new party.

The alleged ethnic character of the party (coupled with vague allegations of 'treasonable activities' was indeed the excuse Kaunda used when in September 1971 he imprisoned another one hundred and fifteen UPP leaders. Although Kapwepwe was spared on this occasion, his freedom was to come to an abrupt end when, a few months later, Kaunda locked him up too, together with another one 122 of his colleagues.

It has in recent times been suggested that Kaunda acted as rashly and brutally as he did because some of the UPP supporters had allegedly set fire to a dance hall in the Copperbelt town of Chililabombwe, which resulted in the deaths of 12 people. This explanation is not only spurious, it also has a sequencing problem. The dance hall fire occurred in 1978 whereas the mass UPP detentions took place in 1971. In 1978, the usual suspects from the now banned UPP were rounded up. They included John Chisata, a former unionist and junior minister in the 1960s, and Chinkangala Fostino Lombe, a former teacher who had spent close to a decade as a political prisoner either as a UPP activist or on other vague allegations of attempting to overthrow Kaunda's government.

The principal lawyer for these detainees was Levy Patrick Mwanawasa who in the course of his duties came upon a report on the Chililabombwe fire that appeared to conclude definitively that the tragedy had been caused not by arson, but by an electrical fault. This finding did little to speed up the release of Chisata and Lombe, who were to spend another two years in prison before being finally set free. Sadly, Chisata and Lombe passed away, within a month of each other, in the middle of 2008, only a couple of years after finally receiving an apology and compensation from the State for their arbitrary imprisonment. Their lawyer, Levy Patrick Mwanawasa, who had become president of the republic in 2001, died on August 19, 2008.

The detentions under the infamous Preservation of Public Security Act were not supported by formal charges. Thanks to the referendum of 1969, Parliament had little oversight over this overt breach of human rights. The law requiring states of emergency to be reviewed by parliament every six months, had now been scrapped, effectively placing the country in a permanent state of emergency; a paradise for any leader with autocratic ambitions.

It was in this political climate that President Kaunda announced a commission of enquiry in March 1972 to establish *the nature* Zambia's one party state was to take. There was of course no need for a referendum. The population was not being asked whether they wanted a one party state. That decision had already been taken, contrary to Kaunda's promise in 1964 that a single party system of government would only come about in Zambia through the ballot box. Now he appointed a commission, led by the affable lawyer and politician, Mainza Chona, to consult the population, by way of public hearings and submissions, on the best way of implementing a one party state other than through the ballot box.

The Chona Commission, as it came to be known, did a good job in very difficult circumstances. Unfortunately some of the more progressive recommendations they made, like term limits for the president, were disregarded by Kaunda and UNIP.

The first election under the One Party constitution was held on December 5, 1973. Only UNIP candidates were allowed to contest the 136 parliamentary seats, and Kenneth Kaunda was the sole candidate in the presidential election. Voters in the presidential election which was conducted concurrently with the parliamentary election were asked to vote either 'yes' or 'no' for the presidential candidate. In reality the presidential 'election' was more of a referendum than a poll.

There were 1,746,107 registered voters but only 33.4 per cent (or 583,607) of that number actually voted. Of those who voted 56,355 either left their ballots blank or spoilt their vote. The total number of valid votes was therefore only 527,252. This low turn out in a country were the citizenry had previously voted in large numbers, and with enthusiasm, represents a rejection of the one party system of government by the Zambian population. It is fair to say although it had huge power, the one party government lacked legitimacy from inception, as it had been brought into being not only by a minority of Zambians but also a minority of those who had taken the trouble to register as voters.

The successful parliamentary candidates celebrated their victory over fellow party members. Even though he was the only presidential candidate, President Kaunda was also jubilant at his overwhelming percentage victory.

Detention without trial

The cases of Justin Chimba, one of Zambia's first cabinet ministers, Robinson Puta, businessman and founding Chairman and Chief Executive Officer of Zambia Railways Board, John Chisata, Jameson Chapoloko, an ardent campaigner for Zambian independence, William Chipango, former mayor of Livingstone, Musonda Chambeshi, trade unionist and official of the United Progressive Party, and Simon Mwansa Kapwepwe, have been reasonably well documented and commented upon by practitioners and students of constitutional law. All of these people were arbitrarily imprisoned and many of them tortured during the second republic.

These men however had a high profile in society and it could be said that status accorded them some protection from the excesses of the Kaunda regime. I was to discover more about human rights abuses when I myself was imprisoned in connection with my work as a human rights lawyer. I could see how people who did not have much in the way of societal clout were vulnerable to unrestrained abuse. Morris Kapepa was one such person.

Kapepa was 76 years old when I met him in 1981. He was in prison on a detention order signed by President Kaunda. Kapepa had been administratively accused of having links to a person considered by many to have been Zambia's most notorious dissenter, Adamson Bratson Mushala, whose rebellion lasted from 1975 to 1982.

Mushala was initially a UNIP loyalist and prior to Zambia's independence was sent to China for guerrilla training with a view to coming back to overthrow the colonial government. But Mushala did not return to Zambia until after the end of colonial rule and establishment of the first indigenous government. He was not alone in the UNIP leadership to hold a strong sense of entitlement to a good job in the new government. Accordingly Mushala asked to be given the job of chief warden in the forestry department. Mushala's request was turned down by the UNIP government. He reacted to what he saw as rejection, with frustration and anger and decided to join an opposition group, the United Party, founded by another unhappy UNIP leader, Nalumino Mundia.

Mushala may well have been content to attack the government in his new role as member of an opposition party, within the constitutional framework. Unfortunately, the United Party was banned and Mushala decided to flee to South Africa with a band of followers. In 1975, he transformed his group into a combat force and returned to Zambia to wage a campaign of terror, mostly in the northwest. That campaign continued sporadically until November 26, 1982 when security forces gunned him down.

Mushala's second in command, Alexander Saimbwende, took over the reins but was generally considered less effective than Mushala. He appeared to have difficulty directing his band of followers, and undermining the UNIP government, with his campaign being more sporadic and erratic than Mushala's. On September 25, 1990 Saimbwende surrendered to Alexander Kamalondo, UNIP's political leader in the North Western Province.

In the meantime many people, primarily from the North Western province, had been detained on suspicion of supporting what came to be known as the Mushala gang. It was difficult to imagine many of these detainees as wagers of terror, and in the case of Morris Kapepa, impossible to do so.

At the time of his arrest, Kapepa was employed on a commercial farm on the Chingola-Solwezi road. He appears to have been in semi retirement because his employers, a white Zambian family, were unwilling to let him go completely. They had found him trustworthy and reliable. So he continued to live on the farm.

One day in 1977 officers from Zambian security forces showed up at the farm as part of a campaign to seek out and arrest Mushala sympathisers. The workers were assembled and asked to provide any information they might have about the terrorist group. No one had any useful information to offer. The workers were then asked to produce their UNIP cards. Those who had the cards produced them. Mr. Kapepa however was unable to do so, as he had not belonged to a political party for many years. He did however remember that he kept an old African National Congress card with his important papers, so he produced that. That was enough to make him a person of interest to the security forces.

Kapepa was taken away to Kamfinsa prison in Kitwe where he was interrogated at length. The interrogators got nothing from him and decided that he was hiding important information. In order to make him talk, the officers resorted to an old tactic - torture. Mr. Kapepa was beaten and then suspended from a tree. At this point a statement was written by one of the officers who told Mr Kapepa that he could end his suffering simply by signing the statement. He was wise enough to know that he was in effect being accused of treason and that the consequences of admitting to such a crime could be dire. He therefore declined to sign.

It was at this point that Morris Kapepa was stripped naked and subjected to gruesome torture concentrated on his testicles. In fact one of Kapepa's testicles was crushed, threatening his very life. It was clear to all that Kapepa needed urgent medical treatment. But the security officers would not allow him to go to hospital until he signed the statement written for him. In the end Morris Kapepa had no choice but to sign the piece of paper. After his surgery, Kapepa was imprisoned at Mpima State Prison in Kabwe.

When I met Morris Kapepa as a fellow prisoner he was already in his seventies, hunched over, and walked rather slowly. He kept himself busy by weaving baskets, an art that he and the other "Mushala" detainees had mastered perfectly. Kapepa had very few visits because his wife could not afford the bus fare from Chingola to Kabwe, on a regular basis. She only managed to see him about once every six months. Despite this, Kapepa always appeared dignified, and totally without bitterness. He did however often ask those who had met Kenneth Kaunda whether the President was entirely human. The question was not provoked by anger but rather by sad curiosity. Kapepa could not understand how anyone could be so callous about another's life. Morris Kapepa spent six years in prison without trial, before he was finally released to rejoin his elderly wife and family.

Another detainee who would have been justified to ask the question about the President's humanity was Joseph Sanken. Joseph had also been detained on suspicion of belonging to the Mushala gang. He was arrested with a childhood friend when they had gone into a bush near their village where they grew crops. Both were completely illiterate at the time of their arrest. But the skill they displayed in making baskets with intricate patterns, and the speed with which Joseph had picked up the Nyanja language, suggest the two detainees were far from unintelligent. I never found out the ages of Sanken and his friend Chipawa but my guess was that they were in their thirties, with Sanken being the younger of the two.

Joseph Sanken was a stout, frankly curious, and obliging sort of fellow who avoided challenging the authorities, unless the matter had to do with his food rations. Joseph's philosophy was that people came into the world to suffer and whatever happiness they enjoyed could be no more than a respite from the central mission of misfortune. Chipawa on the other hand was short, slim, quiet and ambitious. He did not seem to share Joseph's sense of fatalism but assumed that life could be much better and that there might be a future for him despite his current circumstances. Chipawa learnt to read and write while in detention. Joseph did not.

It is perhaps for this reason that Joseph did not realise for a long time that his detention may have been unlawful, even by the standards of the draconian Preservation of Public Security Regulations.

When a state of emergency is declared in Zambia, the law requires the president to apply his or her mind to the act of detaining a person. But the practice in the Second Republic (as the one party state era is known) was for the president to pre sign blank detention orders. So, when Joseph Sanken was given his detention order, the security officer arresting him needed only to insert Joseph's name. Joseph was informed that he was going to prison and told to wait. While waiting for his fate, another security officer reviewed Joseph's case and decided to issue a pre signed Revocation of Detention Order. But someone forgot to tell Joseph he was free to go. He waited at the police station where he was held until all detainees were transferred to prisons. When he arrived at Mpima State Prison, the authorities there were shown Joseph's original detention order, and on that basis admitted him as a political prisoner.

Speaking a mixture of Bemba and Nyanja, the main Zambian languages, I did eventually explain to Joseph that his detention could be challenged.

On the basis of these contradictory orders, I agreed to draft a petition to the tribunal that reviewed detentions after the petitioner has been incarcerated for one year or more. Joseph had been in prison for about three years and was therefore eligible. Unfortunately, thanks to the Referendum of 1969, the tribunal could not order a detainee's release; its powers now limited to merely recommending a release. The state routinely ignored these recommendations and it often took years before a person detained under the notorious regulations was released.

I was released before Joseph but I subsequently learnt that he too had been finally allowed to return to his family in the North Western Province of Zambia. We can only hope that he was able to pick up the pieces and move on.

Arbitrariness and callousness was not confined to human rights. Economic laws too were disregarded, all leading to the conclusion that for most of her modern history Zambia has not been governed well. The exception to the rule would be the first four years of independence when the country recorded great economic growth and was routinely compared to the more impressive tiger economies of Asia. Despite occasional political hiccups, the country was relatively well run during this period because it had a professional, independent, and merit-based civil service that was able to implement policy crafted by politicians. The civil service was also able to guide these politicians appropriately.

Unfortunately there was no commitment to democracy and as soon as the new rulers had the confidence to do so, plans were made to convert the country into a dictatorship. Political decline usually leads to economic decline, and this is what happened in Zambia after the institution of the one party system of government. There were of course other factors, such as the commodities price slump and the oil shocks of the 1970s that contributed to economic decline. The point is however that a democratic Zambia would have been better equipped to deal with these external factors than an inefficient one party state. For one thing a democratic system would have allowed for alternative views which may well have mitigated some of the harsher consequences of the fall in copper prices and the oils shocks.

It has to be concluded that the one party system of government set the cause of both political and economic development back. The Second Republic was not Zambia's finest hour. The political excesses of that era have been discussed in this chapter. The next chapter will look at the country's economic decline and how this was compounded by the political system of the day.

CHAPTER 2

A SOUTHWARD BOUND ECONOMY

Post-independence economic policies

When Zambia attained independence in 1964, the country's formal economy was almost entirely controlled by foreign investors. The manufacturing sector was limited to the production of items needed by the giant mining industry on a daily basis, or consumer items such as beverages that could not reasonably be imported.

Although the much disliked Federation of Rhodesia and Nyasaland had been dissolved a year earlier, its influence and structures were still evident in 1964. The British South Africa Company, originally setup by the British imperialist and posthumous philanthropist, Cecil John Rhodes, only relinquished mineral rights purportedly acquired from a concession signed with the Litunga of Barotseland in 1892, on the eve of Zambia's independence. The concession, known as the Lochner Concession, was always going to be legally problematic as the mineral deposits to which the rights conferred on Rhodes by the Litunga related, were in fact located in territory not under the Litunga's jurisdiction. But it was not legality that led to the relinquishing of the rights, it was the threat by the new Zambian government to expropriate the BSAC and remove it entirely from participation in Zambia's lucrative mining industry.

Zambia's history with the British South Africa Company, in particular, and the Central African Federation (1953-1963) in general, was not a happy one. Northern Rhodesia's copper revenues were spent in the country only when it was absolutely necessary to do so; the bulk of the revenues were sent to white dominated Southern Rhodesia, which was considered a much better destination for "British" capital. The conventional wisdom of the time was that Southern Rhodesia was unlikely to have an indigenous government in the foreseeable future, unlike Northern Rhodesia which was showing susceptibility to the wind of change that was already responsible for the conversion of the British colony of Gold Coast to the independent Republic of Ghana.

On this basis, the federal government managed the three territories of the Federation in a way most favourable to Southern Rhodesia. In addition to receiving the bulk of the revenue from copper rich Northern Rhodesia, Southern Rhodesia was also assigned the responsibility of providing managerial and administrative skills. It was also Southern Rhodesia that hosted the Federation's only university. Northern Rhodesia provided copper revenues while Nyasaland was used as a pool of cheap Black labour. When the federal arrangement was over and Zambia had attained independence, the scars of history were everywhere present. The most telling legacy of the colonial experience was in the field of education. Despite having a relatively sophisticated economy, Zambia was left with fewer than 100 university graduates at independence.

The country had an acute shortage of skills and the new nationalist government made it clear that it was "in a hurry" to develop the county and address the skills shortage as rapidly as possible. It is in this context that the adoption of national development plans must be seen. It has been suggested that in adopting national development plans, Zambia was influenced by the Soviet Union and its brand of socialism. In fact the imperatives at play had more to do with nationalism and the simple desire to develop, than the ideology of Marxism and Leninism. At this point in history Kenneth Kaunda was far from being a socialist let alone a communist. He went so far as stating on record that Zambia would not send its soldiers to what was known as the Eastern block of nations for training out of a belief that soldiers sent there were bound to come back confirmed communists. In later years, Kaunda's position was to change but in 1964 he was, to say the least, cautious about communist ideology. So, the Transitional Development Plan (1964-66) was instituted as a nationalistic response to the colonial economic and social legacy. The same is true of the First National Development Plan (1966–71). These two plans provided for massive investment in infrastructure and manufacturing so that by the end of the decade Zambia had a new link to the sea which avoided southern routes controlled by rebel Rhodesia, apartheid South Africa and Portuguese-run Angola and Mozambique. Thanks to the two national development plans, Zambia also developed a reasonably successful motor vehicle assembly industry in the south of the country that initially assembled Fiat cars but later added Peugeot cars and Mercedes trucks to its portfolio. But the expansion of infrastructure and creation of a few more state-owned businesses like the Livingstone Motor Assemblers company did little to address the economic imbalance in the country that left Zambians with very little equity in the key companies of the country. The Zambian government took the view that this imbalance could only be addressed by a major and deliberate restructuring of the economy.

Zambianisation of the Economy

The idea behind the Mulungushi reforms of 1968 was to restructure the Zambian economy so as to reduce foreign domination and increase Zambian participation in the economy. In announcing the reforms to UNIP's National Council at Mulungushi Rock on 19 April 1968, Kaunda made it clear that the reforms were aimed at Zambianising rather than indigenizing the economy. While recognising and welcoming the fact that many non indigenous Zambians had in fact acquired Zambian citizenship, Kaunda lamented the reality of an "appreciably large number of [non indigenous people] who have chosen to remain outside the national family".

It was the failure of economically powerful non indigenous residents to integrate themselves into the Zambian social fabric and protect and promote Zambian economic interests that gave the impetus to the Mulungushi reforms. The reforms were not motivated by Marxism or any other socialist ideology, as so many Western commentators have simplistically concluded. In addition to the intransigence of the settler population, there were other historical and geopolitical factors that made the reforms necessary.

Zambia had a colonial legacy that left the bulk of nationals as mere bystanders in economic matters; the white regime in Southern Rhodesia had committed treason against the United Kingdom by making a unilateral declaration of independence (UDI), and the ruling party in Zambia was rife with political tension as the firebrand Simon Kapwepwe became Vice President of the Republic.

Pre independence Zambia was a segregated society with 'Africans' 'Europeans' and 'Indians' being obliged to live in separate residential areas. Until the end of colonial rule, even mixed race people were obliged to live in certain areas; they could not choose where to live. Europeans did not generally operate businesses in African townships and rural areas where the bulk of black Zambians lived. The areas where Africans were permitted to run businesses in the townships were designated 'second class trading areas'. Europeans carried on business in 'first class trading areas'.

The second class trading areas produced many successful businessmen like Justin Simukonda of Luanshya, Robinson Puta of Bancroft, now Chililabombwe, Luka Mumba of Fort Rosebery now Mansa, Pascale Sokota of Kitwe, Tom Mtine of Ndola, and Safeli Chileshe of Broken Hill, now Kabwe. Other names like Chilaka, Chizema, Kapikila, Kashimbaya, Kazembe, Msiska, Mwenso, Nhekairo, fortified this class of entrepreneurs.

The UNIP government was well aware of this class of businessmen as many of them had contributed to the cause of independence. The African businesses were successful mostly in trading, contracting, and transportation. The Mulungushi reforms aimed at extending this success to a greater portion of the country. Thus the reforms confined non Zambian traders to the old first class trading areas in downtown areas of the main cities and towns, and reserved the rest of the country for Zambians, regardless of their skin colour.

But the reforms went further than simply restricting areas where foreigners could trade. Certain activities were also reserved exclusively for Zambians. For example, building mineral permits for quarrying and brick making were reserved for Zambians. Road transport permits for the operation of buses, taxis, internal freight services were similarly reserved for Zambians or corporations owned at least 75 per cent by Zambians.

Although Kaunda had previously shown his impatience with foreigners who did not wish to integrate themselves into Zambian society, he still delayed implementation of the regulations pertaining to trading licences, mineral permits, and road service permits until the time for renewal of the current permits and licences.

Since the reforms were announced in April and licences were normally renewed at the end of December, this delay in implementation gave those foreigners now inclined to do so, another eight months to apply for Zambian citizenship. For those not inclined to be part of the 'national family' there was ample time to dispose of businesses to Zambian citizens.

It is not clear how many settlers assumed Zambian citizenship as a result of this generous gesture. We can surmise however that the number was miniscule. At the time of the Mulungushi reforms, three and a half years after independence, only 600 whites and Indians had changed their nationality to Zambian. In 1964 the white population stood at 75,000. It is reasonable to assume that not too many of them changed their nationality in the eight months between the announcement of the reforms and the renewal of current licences and permits.

The more famous aspect of the Mulungushi reforms is perhaps the Government's declared intention to acquire equity in a number of key foreign-owned companies. There was a sense at the time that foreign owned companies were doing little to speed up Zambianisation and skill development in their organisations. There was also suspicion that many foreign controlled companies were at best indifferent to the hostile Smith regime in Southern Rhodesia and at worst supportive of the illegal regime that had done so much to undermine Zambian stability. The geopolitics of the time strengthened the hand of economic hardliners at home who wanted immediate and dramatic control of the economy by Zambians.

In pursuance of this desire the government declared its intention to acquire equity holdings (usually 51% or more) in a number of key foreign-owned firms, to be controlled by a state owned conglomerate known as the Industrial Development Corporation, popularly known as INDECO. Ironically INDECO had started life toward the end of federal rule as an agency that promoted private enterprise. But by January 1970, it was being used to acquire majority holding in the Zambian operations of the two major symbols of foreign private enterprise, the Anglo American Corporation and the Roan (formerly Rhodesian) Selection Trust. The two mining giants became known as the Nchanga Consolidated Copper Mines and Roan Consolidated Mines.

In an effort to rationalise the management of state enterprises, the Zambian government then created new state holding companies to be responsible for the mining and finance sectors. These new state companies were known as the Mining Development Corporation (MINDECO) and the Finance and Development Corporation (FINDECO). The joke at the time was that soon all night clubs would be brought under a single corporate entity to be known as SINDECO!

Although FINDECO gained control of insurance companies and building societies, foreign-owned banks (such as Barclays, Standard Chartered and National and Grindlays) successfully resisted takeover and absorption into FINDECO.

More changes occurred in 1971 when INDECO, MINDECO, and FINDECO were brought together under a giant state enterprise known as, the Zambia Industrial and Mining Corporation (ZIMCO), to create a company large enough to have a place in the Fortune 500 rankings. The company was considered so critical to the country's economy that President Kenneth Kaunda himself chaired its board of directors.

About a decade later, NCCM and RCM were merged into the giant Zambia Consolidated Copper Mines Limited ZCCM. The merger followed the controversial termination in 1973 of the management contracts under which day-to-day operations of the mines had been carried out by Anglo American Corporation and Roan Selection Trust. The story of the termination is worth telling as it exemplifies unbridled collaborative high level corruption.

The acquisition by the Zambian government of 51 per cent of the copper mining companies was financed in part by the issuance of interest bearing bonds by ZIMCO. The bonds were to mature, in the case of RST in 1978 and in the case of AAC in 1982. In both cases the bonds attracted an interest rate of six per cent per annum. These bonds were eventually placed on the market by the principal holders, and according to Andrew Sardanis, writing in *Africa: another Side of the Coin,* by the middle of 1973 were trading at a discounted rate of between 50 and 55 per cent.

There was a businessman who was watching the performance of the bonds very carefully. Roland "Tiny" Rowland the British businessman and chairman of the London Rhodesia Company, better known as Lonrho, did not enjoy the early part of 1973. Evidence had surfaced that Tiny Rowland had been misusing company funds to support friends and his lavish lifestyle. This led some members of his board of directors to call for Mr. Rowland's resignation. Lonrho had invested significantly in Zambia and in many other African countries.

This fact was largely responsible for Rowland's survival of the boardroom revolt and his continuing as Chief Executive Officer of Lonrho. Tiny Rowland launched an impressive campaign outside the boardroom aimed at convincing the British establishment that if he were ousted, Lonrho assets in African countries would be nationalised. The Zambian High Commissioner to London indeed testified in court, by way of affidavit, to this effect. Tiny Rowland won the day, although he lost the court action and avoided dismissal only because the court left the final decision in the hands of the shareholders, who saved him.

The troublesome directors were all removed from his board. Tiny now had a more compliant board and consequently a freer hand to run his business empire. At one point Tiny referred to his new directors as 'Christmas decorations'. In any event Mr Rowland could once again turn his undivided attention to the performance of the ZIMCO bonds.

Having been saved from ouster by Zambian Government officials claiming to act on behalf of Tiny Rowland's friend, Kenneth Kaunda, the British businessman continued to not only watch the ZIMCO bond market but to purchase them whenever he could.

As soon as the Zambian Government announced that it was redeeming the ZIMCO bonds, Tiny Rowland cashed in his paper, bought at a hugely discounted rate, and got the full residual value of $1.10 per bond.

No rational reason has ever been given for the premature redemption of the bonds. It is clear however that Tiny Rowland and his Zambian Government cronies made a fortune out of this blunder. Sardanis has estimated that Zambia would have saved at least $115 million if the country had bought the bonds itself on the market rather than redeeming them. Now the bulk of that money ended up in Mr Rowland's pocket.

In manipulating the bond market as he did, Tiny Rowland was helped by the fact that these bonds were all issued by one state corporate entity. It would have been much more difficult to persuade privately-owned companies to prematurely redeem the bonds, as this would have involved relatively large unplanned outlays of capital. In contrast, ZIMCO simply turned to the state for the money and by the end of the exercise the national foreign exchange reserves were lowered by the redemption price of $231 million.

Rowland's accomplices were well placed Zambian 'leaders' who evidently did not subscribe to the view that state assets should be managed as prudently as privately-held wealth. Instead they saw these assets as an opportunity for self-enrichment.

Effects of Nationalisation

The failure of the Zambian individual to relate in a personal way to the nationalised companies was to contribute to the ultimate failure of state enterprises. It has to be acknowledged however that state enterprises did provide an opportunity for rapid training of Zambian nationals. It is telling that when eventually these companies were privatised virtually all Zambians in a position to either acquire equity in, or manage the newly privatised entities had received their training from one or other state enterprise. Indeed this was consistent with the original idea of letting the state acquire a controlling interest in key companies, and later offload these shares to members of the Zambian public by way of a favourable floatation at a future Zambian stock exchange. Unfortunately by the beginning of the 1970s when the stock exchange was expected to be established and the state enterprise shares sold to the public, Kenneth Kaunda had discovered socialism. In the event the stock exchange was stillborn and the floatation never took place.

The folly therefore may not have been the idea of state participation itself but rather the naïve belief that nationalised companies could be a permanent feature of the Zambian economic landscape.

The failure of the state enterprise sector to relate positively to Zambian nationals at a personal level is illustrated by the story of Chanda Julius Kabambala. Mr Kabambala is a professional driver. He first worked in that capacity in 1967 after leaving school. He worked for different organisations over the years, including the Lusaka City Council, Zambia National Tourist Bureau, and Eagle Travel. Throughout his working life Mr Kabambala has paid his taxes and also contributed into the Zambia National Provident Fund, which was later renamed National Pension Scheme Authority. His salary in 1967 was K56 (about US$78.40).

Julius, as he is known to his friends, had hoped to retire at the turn of the 21st century, having taken care of all his basic needs and housing requirements. Despite having contributed faithfully to NAPSA and its predecessor organisation ZNPF, Julius found it necessary to continue working in 2008. After working for 35 years, Julius received a lump sum benefit of ZMK 904, 480.17, or less than US$200, in 2002. He was able to purchase a modest house only because of the new government's policy of selling council houses to sitting tenants at a huge discount. Julius now lives in the two-bedroom house.

Chanda Julius Kabambala is in fact a victim of poor management of ZNPF which followed political dictates rather than business criteria in investing. The state enterprise threw money at politically-inspired projects and paid little attention to the long term interests of its members. ZNPF's ability to invest for the benefit of members was further handicapped by the fact that the government often raided its coffers in order to finance the national budget, a huge proportion of which went to emoluments.

Like its insurance counterpart, Zambia National Insurance Corporation, ZNPF did not index link the pension benefits of members. These members, like ZSIC's policy holders, found themselves with substantially less money than they should have, when the final payments were made. In the case of Chanda Julius Kabambala, he received the equivalent of less than three months salary (in 1968 dollars) after contributing for 35 years!

Overall the state enterprises charged with securing the future of members and policyholders failed these members and policyholders and missed an opportunity for wealth creation for ordinary Zambians.

But the nationalisations were also ill timed. Zambia was not an island unaffected by events in the rest of the world. The country's plans for an economy controlled by state enterprises were soon overtaken and adversely affected by events in the wider world. In 1973, while Zambia was preparing for the first one party election, the Organisation of Petroleum Exporting Countries (OPEC) quadrupled the price of oil. This was followed by a slump in copper prices in 1975, resulting in a severe reduction of export earnings. Thus between 1973 and 1975 Zambia's earnings from copper were reduced by 50 per cent while the cost of her main imports skyrocketed. For a while Zambia resisted passing on the increased cost of oil by heavily subsidizing products that used this commodity. Thus food and fertiliser were heavily subsidised. At the same time there was a reluctance to reduce expenditure, as evidenced by the bloating of the public sector. Zambia not only had a cabinet but also, thanks to the newly instituted One Party State, a central committee whose members were, like the cabinet, entirely supported by the treasury. Thus Zambia did not just have a minister for finance; it also had a chairman of the finance committee in the Party central committee.

Instead of closing the gap between imports and exports by cutting public spending Zambia resorted to heavy borrowing, mostly from the Bretton Woods institutions, like the International Monetary Fund (IMF).

Zambia was losing control of the economic development agenda and it was not long before the Third National Development Plan (1978–83) was abandoned, as crisis management was substituted for long-term planning. By the mid-1980s Zambia had become one of the most indebted nations in the world certainly when the country's total debt stock was compared to the national gross domestic product.

Zambia looked to the IMF for help but it would only help at a price. It insisted that the Zambian government introduce programmes, known as structural adjustment programmes, aimed at bringing stability to the economy and restructuring it so as to reduce dependence on copper. The IMF also of course wanted the country to be well placed to pay back future and past loans. The IMF conditions for lending money to Zambia: ending of price controls; devaluation of the local currency; reductions in government expenditure; removal of subsidies on food and fertilizer; and raising producer prices for farmers so as to increase agricultural output. These were all meant to restore macro economic balance and help the country pay back its debts.

The removal of food subsidies however was not without risk. When Kenneth Kaunda removed the subsidies, there was of course a huge increase in the price of food including the staple maize meal. The country's urban population that consumed most of the staple food protested and many of them took to the streets in uncharacteristic fashion, and rioted.

The Zambian leadership was shocked by the extent of the rioting and in desperation the Kaunda government broke with the IMF in May 1987 and replaced the proposed IMF structural adjustment programme with a home grown New Economic Recovery Programme in 1988. NERP was not a resounding success and by 1989 Kaunda was again asking the IMF for help.

The rapprochement was perhaps inevitable given the weakening and eventual collapse of communism in the Soviet Union and Eastern Europe (which had provided, albeit to a limited extent, an alternative source of funding for Kaunda's regime).

The supremacy of capitalism became unquestionable in 1990 and with that came a renewed reverence for the Bretton Woods institutions.

Meanwhile patience for Kaunda and his dictatorial system of government was running out at home. Dissent became more open and initially quite unfocused. The dissenters who included men and women from all walks of life could not form opposition parties. They could however form civic organisations. This is precisely what they did in early 1991 when an unlikely coalition of businesspeople, trade unionists and other civic leaders came together to form an organisation called the Movement for Multiparty Democracy. The aim of this organisation was to lobby the government to reintroduce democracy. The MMD was successful in its efforts and by the middle of the year had registered itself as a political party. Before the end of the year, the coalition which included former members of the United Progressive Party, the African National Congress and other proscribed organisations, resoundingly won elections and formed a government. On November 2, 1991 a former trade unionist called Frederick Chiluba became president of the republic.

Chiluba grasps the nettle

President Chiluba understood that if long term progress was to be made in Zambia the distortions of the command economy had to be rectified as quickly as possible. He knew that doing so would not be painless. Indeed he had taken the politically unusual step during the campaign of constantly reminding his audience at public meetings that they would endure pain before progress could be made. The audience always accepted the price and seemed to believe that nothing could be worse than the Kaunda regime from which they were about to be liberated.

Thus the Chiluba government committed itself to extensive economic reform. Perhaps the bravest decision taken by the Chiluba administration was to repeal restrictive exchange control regulations which tightly (and ridiculously) controlled the export of currency from Zambia. During the Kaunda years, it was not unusual for people who had sent money abroad outside the framework of this colonial-era law to be imprisoned and fined huge amounts for flouting exchange control regulations. Young people returning abroad to school (after spending holidays in Zambia with their parents) in possession of 50 pence coins usually got away with confiscation and a reprimand.

Although the rate of inflation during the last years of Kaunda's rule was very high, interest rates remained relatively low. When Kaunda stepped down in 1991, inflation stood at 100 per cent. The high trend continued under President Chiluba, reaching a peak of 180 per cent in 1993 before dropping to 20 per cent in 2001. The Mwanawasa regime continued with the monetarist policies initiated by Chiluba and saw inflation drop to below 10 per cent in 2004. In 2007 the rate was as low as eight per cent. Alas, owing to the global spike in food and energy costs, inflation was soon back in double digit territory, standing at 15 per cent in November 2008. The rate did get back to below 10 per cent in mid 2010.

During Kaunda's rule, depositors did not receive positive returns on their savings, considering themselves fortunate when they were paid 10 per cent per annum. This meant that for every $100 deposited in a savings account in 1991, over a period of one year, the 'saver' lost $100 in terms of spending power and against that got $10, for a net loss of $90.

In an effort to maintain positive real interest rates banks in the immediate post-Kaunda era charged as much as 70 per cent per annum in interest and offered an annual return of around 40 per cent on deposit accounts, although treasury bills paid much more than that. Naturally, a number of businesses failed because they lost access to affordable money. One bank reckoned, correctly, that it would not be possible for the majority of its customers to pay back loans at these rates. Consequently that bank practically stopped lending as a matter of policy. This policy was only lifted around 2005.

In the broader economy the high cost of capital continued to be an obstacle to income growth, and therefore prosperity. This problem has continued. According to Elana Lanchovichina and Susanna Lundstrom who did a study in May 2008 for the World Bank, 82 per cent of business owners considered the high cost of capital to be a major or severe obstacle to growth while 54 per cent of business owners identified limited access to finance as a major or severe obstacle to growth. In 2005, the year under consideration, the average interest rate spread (lending minus deposit rate), according to these authors, was 17 per cent; substantially higher than the 3 per cent for Organisation for Economic Cooperation and Development (OECD) countries, and the 11 per cent for sub Saharan Africa (SSA). Even more telling, domestic credit to the Zambian private sector was on average only seven per cent of Gross Domestic product (GDP) between 1999 and 2005. The comparable figures for OECD and SSA were 176 per cent and 62 per cent respectively.

In the early 1990s, Chiluba, like his intellectual godmother Margaret Thatcher, believed that the harsh medicine he was forcing Zambia to take would result in positive economic growth rates and lead to macroeconomic stability. So, in addition to measures already taken, the government embarked on a policy of privatisation of state-owned companies, most of which at this point were operating extremely inefficiently. Privatisation resulted in many employees losing their jobs and a large number of Zambians consequently becoming poorer.

Unemployment was however also exacerbated by other aspects of Chiluba's liberalisation policies. For example, reducing duty on imported goods resulted in even privately-owned factories closing down as it became more economic to simply import goods that had been previously manufactured in Zambia. Previously vibrant industrial areas in towns like Ndola soon began to look like ghost towns. The City of Ndola as a whole, previously known as the manufacturing centre of the Copperbelt province, started to export labour to other parts of the country and abroad as its economy contracted. The city had previously hosted a reasonably labour intensive textile industry that in fact was the third largest employer, after the mining industry and government, in the country. That industry was now all but decimated as duty free second hand clothing from abroad came into the country and displaced clothing previously manufactured locally.

But there was hope after the government privatized the giant state mining company, Zambia Consolidated Copper Mines. The very act of privatisation of this colossus resulted in Zambia saving $1 million a day, which was the cost to the treasury of keeping ZCCM afloat prior to denationalisation. Privatisation also resulted in a resumption of balance of payments support which in the short term helped the government to implement further economic reform.

As Frederick Chiluba's final term in office was coming to an end, most of the reforms had been implemented. The final transfer of ZCCM's assets occurred on March 31, 2000. In addition work had started on two new mines in the North Western province; one of these was a Greenfield project while the other was an old mine that had been abandoned as uneconomic. The Greenfield project is now a small town, while the old mine employs more than 3000 Zambians.

Copper

A year after the final transfer of ZCCM's assets to the private sector, Zambia recorded its first year of increased copper output since the mid

1970s. While the increase in the copper price from 2005 has helped growth in Zambia, it is important to note that the increase in output actually started before the sharp increase in the price of the commodity. Increased production is attributable to more efficient mining methods.

Both the Chiluba and Mwanawasa governments entered into Development Agreements with new mining companies. These agreements provide for incentives to mining companies to acquire formerly state-owned mines that otherwise would have been unattractive to prospective purchasers. Let us remember that at the time of privatisation, ZCCM was losing $1million a day.

This fact tends to be forgotten by critics of the new mining industry in Zambia. The problem is compounded by a lack of knowledge as to the actual content of the development agreements.

For example, one website claims that, "Virtually all of this income from copper passes Zambia by, because of the terrible and likely corrupt 'Development Agreements' made between the neo-liberal MMD, and various Western companies. These Development Agreements specify that the government does not receive any of the profits, that the companies pay no taxes, and that the companies do not need to use local suppliers."

In fact the Development Agreements do not provide a tax holiday to the new mining companies. On the contrary a typical Development Agreement provides for a tax stability period during which the company is expected to pay 25 per cent corporate tax and an additional 0.6 per cent royalty tax based on the value of copper sold. The stability periods are usually for 15 years although one company has a stability period of only seven years.

Overall the mining companies have acted in good faith when complying with their obligations under these agreements. For example, it was always understood that one Canadian mining outfit would not be in a position to make a profit at its largest mine until at least 2009/10. Owing to increased copper prices and operational efficiencies, the company was in fact able to hand a cheque to the Zambian government for $90.5 million in 2006; four years ahead of budgeted schedule. Coincidentally that is the same year that the Zambian government decided to purchase a luxury helicopter for the president.

In 2007 that same company was responsible for the bulk of the taxes the Zambian Government received from the mining sector, with the company paying seven per cent of total revenue collected by Government. In contrast, GE, Microsoft, and IBM, collectively contribute only 0.7 percent of tax payments to the US treasury.

Furthermore a number of the new mines allotted shares in their companies to the Zambian state mining company ZCCM Investment Holdings on a 'free carried' basis. In other words the state company paid nothing for the shares which were not worth much at the time but which by November 2008 had increased in value significantly. The value of the shares in one new company alone is in excess of $100 million.

The Development Agreements outline the rights and duties of the parties. While the government undertakes not to increase taxes during the stability period, the mining companies undertake to use their best endeavours to use local suppliers and to generally support local businesses.

It is simply not true therefore that "These Development Agreements specify that the government does not receive any of the profits, that the companies pay no taxes, and that the companies do not need to use local suppliers." Nevertheless Zambians should continue to be vigilant in an informed way and encourage mining companies to develop comprehensive social responsibility programmes. This is not a difficult exercise as it requires little more than highlighting best practices already in existence.

Enter Mwanawasa

A year before President Chiluba stepped down as president, Zambia qualified for Highly Indebted Poor Country (HIPC) debt relief. The offer of relief depended on the country meeting certain performance criteria, which included privatisation of the state-owned bank Zambia National Commercial Bank. HIPC appeared to be the long term answer to Zambia's debt problem which previously had only been addressed by way of tinkering through balance of payments support.

Completion of HIPC became (at least publicly) a priority for Levy Mwanawasa who succeeded President Chiluba toward the end of 2001. The two finance ministers who served under Mwanawasa, Emmanuel Kasonde and Ng'andu Magande, both undertook to meet the HIPC benchmarks as soon as possible. Despite this public commitment to

HIPC the Mwanawasa government showed less enthusiasm for reform than Chiluba had done.

It is also fair to say that under President Mwanawasa, the civil service (which had been inherited from the One Party era) saw an opportunity to slow down reform. But the Chiluba reforms had gone too far to be significantly slowed down. In any event the reforms were now beginning to have a positive impact on the economy, as evidenced by the increase in per capita income from the late 1990s.

President Mwanawasa had previously promised to reform the civil service itself by introducing entrance examinations for the institution. When he realised the political value of having a civil service whose leadership is appointed by the executive branch, Mwanawasa quietly backed away from his plans to introduce a merit based selection system for the public service.

Not surprisingly, Mwanawasa also failed to reduce the size of the service which throughout his presidency represented 44 per cent of total formal employment. With such a large civil service gobbling up the lion's share of the national budget, Mwanawasa struggled to improve Zambia's social sector delivery systems.

Mwanawasa's public service was suspicious of the reforms undertaken by Chiluba and in the absence of a leader committed to further reform, slid back into the old ways of a command economy. It is perhaps not surprising that in January 2003, the Zambian Government informed the IMF and World Bank that it wished to renegotiate some of the HIPC conditions calling for privatization of the Zambia National Commercial Bank, Zamtel, the national telephone company, and Zambia Electricity Supply Corporation (ZESCO).

Agriculture

The distortions described above have affected every aspect of the Zambian economy including the agricultural sector which represented 20 per cent of GDP in 2000. The historic challenge in this sector has been Government's failure to pay an adequate producer price to farmers. Indeed the rural-urban migration patterns in the immediate post independence era were a result of the fact that even low paid employees in the urban areas earned so much more than peasant farmers. In addition to low producer prices, farmers experienced difficulty accessing credit and inputs, not to mention chronic problems of foreign exchange availability, at least until foreign exchange regulations were abolished in 1992.

Furthermore rural areas, where the bulk of Zambia's staple food is produced, are at a disadvantage compared to urban areas in ability to access basic facilities for a functioning market. According to the Zambian Central Statistical Office, for every 100 households in urban areas with access to public transport, there are fewer than 65 rural households with access to the same facility. For every 100 households in urban areas with access to public phones, there are only 25 rural households. The gap between rural and urban is most striking with respect to access to internet cafes. Whereas 80 urban households have access to this facility, fewer than 20 rural households do.

B Bramilla and G Porto have shown in their work, Farm Productivity and Market Structure: Evidence from Cotton Reforms in Zambia, that there is a correlation between agricultural output and the absence of these basic facilities. In this 2005 study the authors showed that maize output and cotton output were both undermined by the lack of availability of phone lines, lack of availability of reliable transport, and the high cost or lack of availability of finance.

For as long as infrastructure remains underdeveloped it will be necessary to subsidize agricultural output and ensure that farmers receive inputs on time and are able to transport their produce to the market. President Mwanawasa recognised this and it is perhaps not surprising that during his tenure agricultural output increased significantly.

In 2003, one year after Mwanawasa took office, and Mundia Sikatana became Minister of Agriculture, agricultural production grew by 5 per cent. In 2004 the growth rate dipped slightly but at 4.3 per cent was higher than in the pre Mwanawasa days. This growth led to the country's food security position improving significantly as Zambia moved from an overall deficit of 635,000 metric tonnes in the 2002/2003 consumption period to an overall food surplus of 120,000 metric tonnes the next year, and 185,000 metric tonnes in the year after that. During these periods, maize output rose by 92.5 per cent and Zambia became a net exporter of food. On the other hand, imports of food declined by 15.8 per cent in 2003 and by another 20.7 per cent in 2004.

By way of contrast, when Mwanawasa took power in 2002, the food import bill increased 144.8%. The export of food crops like maize contributed to the growth in non-traditional export earnings.

This impressive record in the productivity of the agricultural sector is due to both good weather (i.e. sufficient rainfall) and the innovative initiatives and strategies employed by the government. For example, the Mwanawasa government introduced a 50 per cent input subsidy under the fertilizer support programme for maize production by small but viable farmers, which enhanced farmers' access to fertilizer and seed. The government also instituted a system of early delivery of seed and fertilizer to farmers throughout the country before the onset of rains. The government further encouraged irrigation farming to ensure food production throughout the year, and not just during the rainy season

This increase in output was not confined to maize. Exports of cash crops such as tobacco and cotton lint also increased noticeably, as did other non-traditional exports like flowers. Non-traditional exports are now mitigating Zambia's dependency on the mining industry in the drive for finding new ways of earning foreign exchange.

Even so, Zambian agricultural development has a long way to go. According to the Thomson Reuters Foundation, Zambia uses only 10 per cent of its more than 40 million hectares of arable farmland. Huge tracts of land remain uninhabited. This assessment was made in October 2008. Clearly Zambia has not begun to tap into its immense agricultural potential.

Expanding the agricultural sector is probably the most effective way of minimising poverty, given the large number of Zambians engaged in the sector.

It is certainly a more effective way of spreading wealth than the Mulungushi reforms which while providing an opportunity for a few nationals to learn the ropes of business, failed to bring about widespread and sustainable economic empowerment.

It is a matter of record that only people who were either loyal to Kaunda and UNIP or were seen as not threatening to the establishment were given positions of responsibility in state enterprises. It was certainly the expectation that officers of the 'parastatal' sector, as the collection of state enterprises were known, should support and enforce the policies of the 'Party and its Government.'

When Valentine Shula Musakanya, who has gone down in history as the country's most able civil servant, showed too much independence in his position as governor of the Bank of Zambia, he was promptly dismissed for having views that were incompatible with Party and Government policy. The Cambridge-educated central banker quickly found more lucrative employment and went on to become a successful businessman in his own right. But not many public servants had Musakanya's options in those days. Many executives working in state enterprises went to extraordinary lengths to prove their loyalty to Kaunda and UNIP in order to maintain their positions. Kaunda's promise in the 1960s that it would pay to belong to UNIP had come to pass.

Unfortunately, blind loyalty does not guarantee ability and soon state enterprises became synonymous with nepotism, corruption and incompetence. The corruption appears to have been encouraged by lack of security of tenure and the unceremonious and humiliating way in which state enterprise chiefs were often removed from their jobs.

Whatever its origins, corruption was real. Commenting on the ZIMCO bonds saga, Andrew Sardanis has observed that a named civil servant who had previously not had much money was suddenly able to offer more than $20 million for a trading group that was having political challenges in Zambia. The offer was made shortly after Tiny Rowland had made a fortune from the premature redemption of ZIMCO bonds. The civil servant in question had played a role in persuading the Zambian government to redeem the bonds prematurely.

It is difficult to imagine a properly run private company agreeing to an early redemption of bonds that would cost it so much. But the state enterprises of the time did not allow themselves to be constrained by the niceties of good corporate governance. In any case they did not have the independence to act like normal corporate entities. They were in effect puppets of the state. It is worth recalling that President Kaunda himself was the Chairman of the ZIMCO board.

Kaunda's chairmanship of the ZIMCO board and his ability to hire and fire other state enterprise chiefs as he saw fit, suggests that merely nationalising companies did not democratise the economy, and may not even have empowered nationals, although it exposed a lucky few to a life of luxury during their tenure.

What is required in Zambia is not nationalisation of industry but rather democratisation of the economy. Zambia needs an economy that affords real opportunities to all citizens regardless of their political affiliations. This economy would be vibrant, diverse, and provide real opportunities for Zambian entrepreneurs to add value to goods and services, whether locally produced or not.

The Mulungushi Reforms did not do this. These reforms succeeded only in creating a new form of state capitalism that still operated in the context of an economy dependent on one commodity for export earnings; an economy that relied on the outside world for importation of virtually all finished goods. The new order also undermined the idea of good corporate governance as state enterprises were shielded from scrutiny, and given the ability by the one party system of government to operate without meaningful regulation. Most state enterprises were monopolies, and this fact helped them to ignore the market which now became dependent on them.

But the nationalised companies were not all-powerful. Even they could not defy economic reality. In the context of a one party system of government with a rigid exchange control system, the state enterprises were, like most other businesses in the country, starved of both local and foreign capital. The absence of a stock exchange at the time and the shortage of savings in the economy brought on by negative interest rates, resulted in a critical shortage of local capital, while rigid foreign exchange regulations denied Zambian businesses access to foreign capital. All this contributed to the poor growth rates seen throughout the second republic (1972 to 1991).

The third republic reforms did not however bring immediate prosperity because liberalisation and development are not necessarily complementary. For example, liberalisation allowed Zambians to purchase good quality consumer goods at home. But this was done at the expense of many job losses as locally produced goods became uncompetitive and the factories from which they were made obliged to close.

The modest gains of recent years notwithstanding, it has to be concluded that Zambia's economic performance thus far has been way below potential. A later chapter will discuss ways of democratising Zambia's economy and possibly creating an environment for sustainable development and prosperity.

CHAPTER 3

A FAILURE OF GOVERNANCE

Zambia's ills cannot be cured until we recognise the fact that this richly endowed country has been poorly managed for most of its existence. As indicated in the Introduction, Zambia's decline has not been merely economic; it has also been moral and political, with all the attendant cultural overtones.

The post independence era has seen the erosion of Zambian traditional culture of mutual support and the emergence of a culture of neglect and avarice. Political structures, designed for the purpose of advancing individual political agendas, have generally failed to provide genuine democratic expression to the people as a whole. Instead they have been used by unprincipled politicians as vehicles for self enrichment or economic security.

Whereas Simon Mwansa Kapwepwe resigned as vice president of the country on principle in the late 1960s and Levy Patrick Mwanawasa also resigned the same position on principle in 1994, it is virtually impossible today to imagine any politician wilfully forgoing the perks of office on principle. The tendency now is for politicians to hang on to public office almost at any cost. For those in the Opposition there is a preoccupation with being noticed by the ruling party leadership in the hope of securing an appointment. In the circumstances party loyalty has been weakened as politicians crisscross back and forth between political parties in search of financial reward. A casualty of this tendency has been the development of party ideology, which cannot crystallise in the absence of a solid and loyal leadership prepared to stand by the party over a long period of time.

This is in contrast to the behaviour of men such as Harry Mwaanga Nkumbula, the only leader of the Opposition during the first republic, and Lawrence Chola Katilungu, the famed trade unionist who also served as vice president of Nkumbula's ANC, but died before Zambia attained independence.

When Zambia was poised to abandon democracy and become a one party state, the African National Congress had little choice but to be incorporated into the ruling UNIP. The terms of incorporation were settled in a document known as the Choma Declaration. Nkumbula, as leader of the ANC, could rightly have expected a position in the UNIP government. Instead Nkumbula declined to serve because he did not believe in UNIP's ideology. He declined the honour for the same reason that Katilungu had declined invitations to abandon the ANC and join UNIP in the late 1950s.

This kind of principle is rarely demonstrated in today's Zambia where the emphasis on personal aggrandisement has legitimised greed and led to a culture of corruption. Sadly no Zambian government has shown the necessary commitment to good governance and transparency, to end this tendency. Zambia is yet to be governed with equity. Lip service has of course been paid to the fight against corruption, with the most convincing campaign against wanton greed being mounted by the late President Mwanawasa. But as we shall see later, even under Mwanawasa there was no commitment to the kind of institutional reform that would guarantee transparency and equity, and truly empower Zambians and engender a sense of personal responsibility among citizens.

Thus far all Zambian governments have abused their power to fight corruption by targeting only their political opponents. As Kenneth Kaoma Mwenda has observed in his book, *Legal Aspects of Combating Corruption: the Case of Zambia*, there has been a tendency to be selective in the prosecution of people suspected of corruption. This has led to inconsistency in the execution of the fight against corruption, which in turn, according to Mwenda, makes it necessary for other actors to join the fight in order to maintain the necessary political will.

Strong and independent institutions are also necessary to ensure fairness and consistency in the fight against corruption. In Zambia, the lack of political will has not only resulted in some culprits not being prosecuted but also in those convicted avoiding punishment and even being glorified. This is perhaps borne out of a culture that treats political allies as a cut above the rest of the population; a culture consistent with slogans like, 'It pays to belong to UNIP'. In this context, one of the rewards of belonging to the right political club is the modification or suspension of inconvenient rules and laws that other citizens have to put up with.

The First Republic

The Case of Henry Shamabanse

Henry Shamabanse was a Minister of State for the Central Province in the mid 1960s. He was then appointed to the corresponding position in the Southern Province and by virtue of that position became the Chair of the Southern Province African Farming Improvement Fund or SPAFIF as it was commonly known. SPAFIF was controlled by a board of directors consisting of Mr Shamabanse, as chair, and other members appointed by him from time to time.

The purpose of SPAFIF was to promote better farming methods among African farmers in the Southern Province. This was typically done by the provision of loans for the execution of eligible projects. For example, SPAFIF would provide finance for projects such as dams, roads, storm drains and other works beneficial to area farmers. At one point SPAFIF had a policy to lend only to groups of farmers rather than individuals. That was certainly the case in June 1968. Five months later the policy changed and SPAFIF was allowed to once again lend to individual farmers.

Mr Shamabanse owned a farm in the Central province which he wanted to improve. In November 1968 when the SPAFIF board was once again able to lend to individuals, Mr Shamabanse wanted to borrow money for the development of his own farm. He decided to do so by obtaining two loans in the amount of Zambian Kwacha 7,500 (about US$8,000 at the time) in the name of a man called Benkele. This was in violation of the African Farming Improvement Funds Act which restricted the granting of loans "to farmers in the area for which the Board has been established"; in this case the Southern Province. Mr Shamabanse also obtained a loan of US$5,500 through the agency of an intermediary company at a time when the board policy was not to lend to individuals.

He was charged on three counts of corruption in respect of the three loans and convicted in the magistrate's court on all counts. He appealed to the High Court where all three convictions were quashed. Unhappy with the High Court's decision, the Director of Public Prosecutions appealed to the Supreme Court. The Supreme Court acquitted Mr Shamabanse on a technicality with respect to the counts relating to the loans amounting to $8,000, but convicted him on the count relating to the $5,500 loan. Shamabanse was sentenced to eight months imprisonment with hard labour.

The Shamabanse case was one of the earliest cases of corruption in Zambia, and how this politician was treated was to influence the fight against corruption in future years. Mr Shamabanse never served his prison term because President Kaunda quickly pardoned him. He went further and reappointed him as Minister of State, this time in the North Western Province.

The clear message from Kaunda was that different rules would apply for those with connections to the ruling elite. The president's action did nothing to discourage corruption. It did however assure potentially and actually corrupt leaders that in times of difficulty they could count on the president for help, as long as they were loyal to Kaunda and his ruling party. Once again it paid to belong to UNIP.

Institutional Corruption

The even sadder fact is that there were other politicians who were more corrupt than Mr Shamabanse who were never charged with any crime. The greed of these politicians is still evident today in the form of industrial monuments which stand as white elephants with only limited benefit to the Zambian population. An example of this is the Indeni 'refinery' which in fact is not a refinery but a series of tanks that does nothing more than separate a cocktail of fuel mixed abroad. The original intention was to construct an oil refinery with the capacity to take in crude oil and refine it. Some of the bureaucrats and politicians given the task of constructing the refinery at Ndola clearly took a cheaper option and pocketed the 'saving' made.

A negative consequence of nationalisation was the fondness that managers of state enterprises developed for imported materials. Not infrequently these imports turned out to be entirely unnecessary and costly. A good example of this is Zambezi Sawmills Ltd which Simon Zukas, the white Zambian nationalist who served on the board of INDECO has analysed in his autobiography *Into Exile and Back*. Zambezi Sawmills had a teak cutting and processing plant at Mulobezi in western Zambia. The operation was a low tech affair because the size of the market could not justify investment in more sophisticated equipment. In fact business was so bad that the owners of the company distinguished themselves from other private sector businessmen by actively seeking nationalisation. They soon got their wish. INDECO took over the company and soon purchased sophisticated sawing machinery from Germany. The cost of the new equipment and the salaries of the technicians who had to operate it very quickly led to unmanageable losses.

Importation of materials was popular because this provided an opportunity for over invoicing which allowed vendors to pay generous commissions to state company executives, and also to previous owners who found it next to impossible to remit dividends under the draconian foreign exchange regulations.

The insecurity of state enterprise managers who were required to be more obedient to political dictates than economic and commercial requirements helped to fuel corruption which, as pointed out earlier, became rampant in the state enterprise sector. The cause for insecurity is perhaps best illustrated by the well known case of Robert Chiluwe who served as managing director of an INDECO company known as Zambia Steel and Building Supplies Ltd. Chiluwe was formally removed from his position by the president of Zambia for being personally disloyal to Kaunda.

Insecurity and greed on the part of Zambian managers were not however the only reasons for corruption in the state enterprise sector. Quite often state enterprise officials would be offered bribes by companies from Europe. A case in point is the tender for design and supervision of the Tanzania Zambia Oil Pipeline (TAZAMA) which attracted a bid from a joint venture company consisting of two British firms. Convinced that all Zambians could be bribed they offered Lishomwa Muuka, the manager responsible for the project, five per cent of the bid if he guaranteed the British companies' success in the bid process. Unbeknown to the British companies' representative, Mr. Muuka had set up a tape recorder which recorded the perverse conversation and subsequently guaranteed the representative a spell in prison.

Nevertheless the era of nationalised industry and the one party state institutionalised corruption in Zambia and legitimised conflict of interest and greed in business transactions. In the mid 1970s President Kaunda's family trust known as the VERITAS Trust wanted to acquire a hugely profitable electronics company in Lusaka known as City Radio Ltd. After failing to pressure the Zambia National Building

Society to provide bridging finance for this purpose, the Kaunda family turned to the more compliant Zambia State Insurance Corporation which obliged. Thus VERITAS Trust was able to purchase City Radio Ltd. The Trust did not own the electronics company for long however as almost immediately after the acquisition, VERITAS sold the company to Zambia State Insurance Corporation (the very provider of the funds that had enabled VERITAS to purchaser the company) for a much higher price.

There was no public outcry about this obvious conflict of interest. Certainly the Kaunda family saw nothing wrong with the transaction as evidenced by the president's public delight with his accountant whom he described as a 'financial wizard.'

The Second Republic

The principal players in the second republic when Zambia was declared a one party state were essentially the same as in the first republic. The difference between the two systems was that the latter allowed for unbridled corruption as there was no longer an opposition to point out the shortcomings of the government.

The standard of behaviour in public life no longer had a robust relationship with moral acceptability and legal culpability; but was rather determined by what the leader could tolerate. Thus the approach taken by the political leadership in the *Shamabanse* case became the norm.

I remember being asked (as a lawyer) in the early 1980s to have a preliminary discussion with a UNIP official who, it was feared by friends and family, might be charged under the Anti Corruption Act. There were a number of possible charges for this potential client revolving around abuse of office and receiving kickbacks. If convicted, he faced five years in prison.

The first thing that struck me about this case was the obvious conflict of interest inherent in the official positions of the prospective client. He served as mayor of Lusaka (under a different title in second republic parlance), sat on the UNIP central committee, and had a day job as chief executive officer of the state building society.

Almost all parcels of land in the City of Lusaka were then, as they are today, allocated to prospective builders by the Lusaka City Council. Successful applicants for the plots would then turn to the state building society for mortgages to allow them to construct homes or other premises on the pieces of land allocated by the council. So, my prospective client not only had political power as a member of the UNIP central committee, the highest policy making body in the country, he also controlled the allocation of plots distributed for development, in addition to allocating funds for the development of these plots.

He certainly had the opportunity to abuse his office and become exceedingly rich in the process. I therefore worried that there might be something to these allegations. But I was also curious as to what his view of the allegations might be. So I took advantage of a previously planned business trip to Lusaka to see the city's leader. We had agreed that we would meet after lunch at his residence. Although I knew the general area where he lived I had never been to his home before, so I allowed a fair amount of time for the trip from my meeting in downtown Lusaka to the mayor's residence.

It was just as well I had done this because it took me a while to locate the actual house. I had in fact gone past the house several times and it was only after seeking directions that I realised that the building I had mistaken for a small block of flats was in fact the house I was looking for.

The mayor greeted me warmly and suggested that we conduct our conversation outside, sitting on a garden swing on the well manicured front lawn of the house. He was no doubt conscious of the possibility that his house might be bugged. A bottle of South African sparkling wine was also offered. Although Zambia was at the time a staunch supporter of sanctions against the apartheid state, it was not uncommon to find South African beverages and other items in the homes of political and business leaders. On this occasion it was South African wine that lubricated the conversation.

The politician told me that the allegations arose from a number of properties that he had developed around the city, with his latest residential construction near the Lusaka Agricultural Showground sparking the investigation. With a mixture of impatience and irritation he opined that the house causing all this trouble was nothing to write home about. It was not even as large as his current residence "which has fourteen rooms".

Toward the end of the conversation I asked the building society chief if he was worried that he might in fact be charged. His response was clear. No one could touch him, he declared calmly. "I know too much about my fellow members of the central committee", he concluded. The transition from prospective to actual client never happened on this occasion. My interlocutor was never charged with any crime. Preferring charges was clearly not in the interests of the political elite.

Human Rights Abuses

Corruption was only one aspect of maladministration in the second republic. Despite Kenneth Kaunda's public commitment to his philosophy of humanism which purported to place "man at the centre of human endeavour", the one party era saw a huge erosion of human rights. The philosophy of humanism was not of course a well thought out coherent doctrine on governance. In reality it represented little more than random thoughts that had been entertained from time to time by the leader of the day. Nevertheless the philosophy did provide a clear theoretical commitment to the protection of human dignity and general enhancement of human rights. Alas the chasm between theory and practice made it irrelevant in the way Zambians were governed.

For almost the entire era of the second republic, Zambia had political prisoners held in poorly serviced prisons without trial. The end of 1971 saw scores of leaders of the new United Progressive Party opposition imprisoned without trial. A year later when the constitution was amended with a view to banning opposition parties, at least 150 people were imprisoned without charge or trial under the notorious Preservation of Public Security Regulations. Fresh detentions for the year 1973 were 160.

This picture continued until July 1, 1990 when an army officer identifying himself as Lieutenant Mwamba Luchembe intermittently broke into the soft music broadcast of Radio Zambia from 3:30 A.M. to about 6:30 A.M., saying the army had taken power. Luchembe cited the food riots of the previous week, in which at least 27 people had been killed and more than 100 wounded, as the reason for the coup.

In the hours after dawn, when it appeared briefly that the coup was successful, Zambians gathered in the centre of the capital city to celebrate the downfall of Kenneth Kaunda. The mood then changed to disappointment when Luchembe was arrested by loyalist troops sent to the radio complex, about four hours after his announcements had begun.

Nevertheless the failed coup attempt against President Kenneth Kaunda further weakened the leader's political standing, already shaky after three days of food riots on the Copperbelt. Although praised abroad by the anti-apartheid movement for his outspoken stance on South Africa, Kaunda was at that time increasingly derided at home as an incompetent dictator.

Every ordinary citizen was affected by the hardship brought on by Kaunda's incompetence. But vocal dissent was limited because of the vast powers that Kaunda had of dealing with opponents. This also explains the abnormally large number of people imprisoned during the Kaunda years. The view that every ordinary citizen was affected by the economic crisis and that there was widespread but silent support for change is perhaps evidenced by the fact that during the three days of rioting, truckloads of paramilitary personnel were seen giving a thumbs-up sign as an indication of support for the protesters.

The story of the Luchembe coup is fascinating and deserves far more analysis than it has received. For our purposes however it must suffice to use the episode as the turning point in the fight against arbitrary detention in Zambia.

The Luchembe coup attempt and the manner in which it was greeted did two things. First, it demonstrated to the Kaunda regime that the one party state was not popular and that there was latent opposition to it. Second, it dented President Kaunda's confidence and left him quite shaken.

It is telling that although Kaunda, who was visiting the Copperbelt Province to open the Zambia Trade Fair in Ndola, went through with his plans, he took the first opportunity to seek solace in religion. After giving a speech contrived to be defiant he broke into a Bemba language hymn, *Lesa E Kachema Wandi* (The Lord Is My Shepherd).

The president's action in the immediate aftermath of the coup attempt revealed the state of anxiety within the Government. Kaunda announced that he was releasing all political prisoners, including Edward Jack Shamwana, the respected lawyer who had been convicted of treason in connection with the 1980 coup attempt. (Valentine Shula Musakanya, the cerebral former governor of the Bank of Zambia who had allegedly colluded with Shamwana to overthrow Kaunda's government, had earlier been acquitted of treason by the Supreme Court.) So prisoners who had been a threat to public security a few days earlier now ceased to be such a threat, and it took a coup attempt for Kaunda to realise this.

The Luchembe coup attempt also hastened plans to reintroduce democracy in Zambia. The joke in the country was that the young lieutenant had done more during his four hour 'presidency' than the government and the underground opposition had managed to achieve in nineteen years of one party rule!

There was a class of people whose fate was even worse than imprisonment without trial. A number of people were tortured and died while in the custody of the police or immigration officers. One of these was Warrant Officer Yotamu Nyirenda who had been arrested under the notorious Preservation of Public Security Regulations. Nyirenda was not detained at a regular prison. Instead he was kept in a guard room at a military centre known as the Arrackan Barracks. The authorities were obviously unwilling to remove the officer from their custody. They therefore arranged for the guardroom to be gazetted as a prison, thereby getting round the difficulty of holding a prisoner in an unauthorised place.

In its September 1995 report the Zambian Human Rights Commission, established after the end of the second republic, noted as follows on page 35:

> The Commission is aware that by convention police and immigration officers did not carry arms generally. If they did, the arms were not displayed publicly. With the declaration of the State of Emergency, and particularly in the Second Republic, however, police officers in particular started bearing arms even when they were on ordinary patrol duties which did not require their being armed. This practice has resulted, in a number of instances, both accidental and deliberate in the shooting of members of the public. The incidents involving Mr Bernard Mutale, Mr Collins Sinkonde deceased and Mr Masauso Banda are some of the cases in point.

In addition to these findings by the Human Rights Commission, there has been for a long time suspicion that certain people who had died in mysterious circumstances during the second republic, had in fact been eliminated for political reasons. The names most often mentioned in this regard are those of Archbishop Elias Mutale, the outspoken cleric who never missed an opportunity to criticise the excesses of the second republic, and Berrings Lombe an unapologetic admirer of Harry Mwaanga Nkumbula and one time Provincial Secretary General for the ANC on the Copperbelt. Both the Archbishop and Mr Lombe were involved in inexplicable car accidents.

Since no thorough investigations took place to determine the cause of these accidents, it is impossible to say with certainty that the state had a hand in these deaths. It is nevertheless an indication of the atmosphere of fear and suspicion that characterised the second republic that to this day the general impression is that Mutale and Lombe were victims of state sponsored terror. The deaths were certainly suspicious.

There is another death associated with the demise of Archbishop Mutale. The archbishop had an associate that allegedly had well placed contacts in the Zambia Security Intelligence Service. That associate was Josephine Mundashi Kapansa. Kapansa was a successful businesswoman who had previously served as a Roman Catholic nun at Lwitikila Mission near Mpika in the Northern Province. According to Beatwell S. Chisala, an author and former diplomat, Archbishop Mutale had visited President Kaunda on the day he was to die. The archbishop told Kapansa that he and Kaunda had had a frank discussion which involved the bishop advising the head of state to return money he had allegedly taken out of Zambia.

After this discussion, the archbishop set off for his home in the prestigious residential area of Roma. He never reached his destination. He was involved in a car accident. Archbishop Mutale did not die immediately. He survived long enough to be taken to the University Teaching Hospital in Lusaka. He was conscious when he arrived at the hospital but no one seemed interested in attending to him despite his pleas. Prophetically, the archbishop warned nurses and doctors passing by that if they did not attend to him soon, he would die and the consequences of his demise would be grave for the country. Eventually, a leader of the Catholic Church making routine rounds at the hospital noticed the injured archbishop and persuaded a doctor to attend to him. It was too late however to save the archbishop who subsequently died from internal bleeding.

A year after the Archbishop's death, Josephine Mundashi Kapansa was also involved in a car accident along the Leopard's Hill road opposite the cemetery. Her car careered off the road and plunged into a gutter. Kapansa was trapped in the car and when help finally arrived, she was already dead.

The case raised suspicion because a month before her death, the former nun had told a number of relations and friends that her movements were being monitored by the Special Branch. On her last day on earth, four men had indeed gone to her house in Woodlands Extension in Lusaka but missed her. The men arrived in a Toyota Land Cruiser, not unlike the ones issued to senior members of Kaunda's Special Branch. They apparently acted in a friendly manner when they talked to Alex Mwamba Mutale, Kapansa's nephew. Mutale was obliging; he gave the men the route Kapansa had taken, and the four strangers followed the businesswoman. The next news Mwamba Mutale got about his aunt was her demise. He was shocked and surprised but his great aunt, Kapansa's mother, while shocked, appeared less surprised. She immediately expressed the view that the state had had a hand in her daughter's death.

Nine years earlier another family had harboured similar suspicions. Berrings Lennox Lombe was kidnapped in Lusaka in October 1982. That was almost exactly two years after Valentine Shula Musakanya and Edward Jack Shamwana had been detained on suspicion of plotting to overthrow Kenneth Kaunda's government. But no connection has been made between Lombe's kidnapping and the alleged coup plot of 1980.

According to Chisala, Lombe left home on the fateful day so he could meet a friend travelling from the Copperbelt city of Kitwe, by bus. He never returned home. The following day Lombe's Datsun 120Y was found abandoned in Kafue. Lombe was not in the car but his clothes were. The search for the missing politician yielded nothing until a senior official in the Kaunda government, Mrs Chibesa Kankasa pleaded to Kaunda for help. Mrs Kankasa was Lombe's cousin. She served as a member of the country's highest policy making body.

After the meeting with Kaunda, Lombe's body was found near Kafue on November 3, 1982. Lombe's relations were convinced, as Kapansa's had been, that the state had had a hand in the death. They brought an action against the state in the High Court but it soon became clear that they were not going to succeed as the pathologist refused to testify. In the circumstances the court had no option but to dismiss the action for lack of evidence.

Although abuse of human rights and economic mismanagement were most egregious in the second republic, the reintroduction of democracy in the third republic has not guarantee good governance either.

The Third Republic

Optimism was everywhere when Kenneth Kaunda was soundly defeated at the 1991 polls and Frederick Chiluba became president of Zambia. Here was a government that had been democratically elected with a huge mandate from the people. Surely with its authority, the Chiluba government would end human rights abuses and corruption; the economy would expand and the shortage of food and other consumer goods would end.

For a while it appeared these hopes would be realised as the Chiluba government moved quickly to reform the economy and end some of the more obvious distortions; shortages of goods soon ended; the permanent state of emergency was automatically ended with the new presidency as the recently appointed Justice Minister, Roger Chongwe, vowed that detention without trial would never again be part of the Zambian political landscape. In due course the mining industry was privatised and tourism expanded.

Within two years of taking office however President Chiluba reacted to what he considered to be politically motivated violence in Lusaka by invoking the hated Preservation of Public Security Act, and imprisoning seventeen opposition leaders without trial. Those detained included Rupiah Bwezani Banda who at the beginning of November 2008 became president of the republic, following the untimely death of President Mwanawasa. Another detainee was Dr Steven Moyo, a respected academic and advocate of transparent government. Chiluba's state of emergency lasted ninety days and the Preservation of Public Security Act was never invoked again. But there was a political casualty from Chiluba's temporary suspension of Zambia's bill of rights; Roger Chongwe, the Justice Minister, felt obliged to resign from the cabinet on account of his earlier promise to do so should the dreaded state of emergency be reinstated.

Chiluba's flirtation with state-sponsored brutality did not however roll back gains made in areas of freedom of speech and assembly. The independent press continued to thrive and opposition parties were generally unrestricted in their activities.

Dictatorship cannot therefore be reasonably said to be the hallmark of President Chiluba's legacy. What seems to be an undeniable part of the former president's legacy is corruption.

Frederick Jacob Titus Chiluba served as the President of Zambia from 1991 to 2001. He was a founding member of the Movement for Multiparty Democracy (MMD) which, under his leadership, ended Kenneth Kaunda's 27-year rule. Chiluba's performance during the first term of his presidency was generally well rated and for this reason he had no difficulty securing a second term in 1996. The second term was however marred by widespread perceptions of corruption. Not surprisingly, President Chiluba's not too thinly disguised attempt to run for an unconstitutional third term met with little support and significant derision and opposition. Zambia's second president had no choice but to respect the constitution. He then devised a way of maintaining influence in the post-Chiluba era by handpicking his one-time vice president Levy Patrick Mwanawasa, as successor to the presidency. The hope was that Mwanawasa would be compliant and allow Chiluba to continue governing, albeit through an intermediary.

It was not to be. Mwanawasa proved more independent than Chiluba had hoped. Within months of taking office, the new president instituted a campaign against corruption and indicated support for the removal of his predecessor's immunity from prosecution.

In February 2003, President Chiluba was charged along with his former director general of intelligence, Xavier Chungu, and several former ministers and senior officials, with 168 counts of theft totalling more than $40m.

The specific allegations against Chiluba were that over his ten-year presidency he had embezzled about $500,000. Like his co accused, the former president was accused of inappropriately using an intelligence bank account known as the Zamtrop account for his personal benefit. The account was held at the London branch of the Zambia National Commercial Bank, then a wholly owned state company.

Proceedings in London

It is perhaps an indication of the difficulty that the state had in proving the theft by public servant charge that the Chiluba matter, despite the national assembly having removed the former president's immunity from prosecution, the legal process soon became moribund and the public began to doubt whether their former president would ever be tried. The former president's supporters pointed to the failure to prosecute the third president as evidence of the unfairness of the charges.

The difficulty of prosecuting Chiluba arose partly because of the general challenge of auditing any intelligence bank account. In this particular case, former president Chiluba had, on the advice of his former intelligence chief, deposited into the Zamtrop account substantial sums of money given to him personally by fellow heads of state and other well wishers. The challenge of convicting Chiluba must have been in Mwanawasa's mind when he made the bizarre offer of ending the trial if Chiluba returned to the state 75 per cent of the money he had allegedly stolen!

Chiluba did not of course take up the offer. In light of this and the stalled criminal proceedings in Zambia, the state now thought pursuing the allegedly stolen assets through English civil courts offered the best hope of returning some of the money to the country. A decision by an English judge finding Chiluba and his co defendants civilly liable would also have the added advantage of boosting the Zambian government's credibility.

And so the Attorney General of Zambia brought the case against Chiluba and 19 of his associates in London. It is unusual in law to conduct a civil case whose fact situation is substantially the same as an ongoing criminal case. The usual practice is for the criminal case to be concluded before the civil matter can commence. The London court must have been aware of this and in an effort not to offend the established practice of waiting for criminal proceedings to conclude before civil proceedings are allowed to commence the presiding judge decided to hold the entire hearing in private. The civil trial opened in London on 31st October 2006 and centred on claims to recover sums which were transferred by the Ministry of Finance between 1995 and 2001.

Chiluba has often claimed that the Zambian government was pressured into prosecuting him by the British government. According to Chiluba the British were very unhappy with him when the Zambian government, under his presidency, rejected a British offer to purchase significant mining assets under the Zambian privatisation programme of the 1990s.

Naturally, Chiluba saw the decision by Mr Justice Peter Smith, the presiding judge in London, to depart from the established practice of not holding a civil trial before the criminal trial had concluded, as evidence of this pressure. On the other hand the judge's unusual ruling to hear the case in private was meant to avoid prejudice to the parallel criminal trial in Zambia. Even so it must have been troubling to Chiluba that the Zambian government's case was funded in part from a $2 million grant given to Zambia for anti-corruption work by the British government.

On 4 May 2007 Chiluba and his co-defendants were found liable for diverting $46 million from the Zambian state. Mr. Justice Peter Smith was not restrained in his criticism of Chiluba's excesses. Although this was a civil case, the learned judge saw Chiluba's free spending as nothing less than theft at a time *"when the vast majority of Zambians were struggling to live on $1 a day and many could not afford more than one meal a day. The people of Zambia should know that whenever he appears in public wearing some of these clothes he acquired them with money stolen from them."*

Chiluba declined to give evidence to the London court. He and his co defendants did however, advance applications to seek a stay of the action. This was done on the basis that

(a) The trial should be postponed until after any criminal trial that might take place in Zambia;
(b) A ring fencing order should be made which prohibited the release or use of any material (including evidence) revealed in the civil trial for any other purpose without the permission of the Court; and
(c) That the defendants could not attend trial in London particularly as the terms of their bail required them to remain in Zambia.

Subsequently, Chiluba intimated in the Zambian press that the London proceedings constituted an infringement of Zambia's sovereign rights and was little more than an attempt by the former colonial power to impose its will upon the Zambians. In blunter moments Chiluba has referred to the judgement as "racist".

Racist or not, it is also undeniable that the former president spent $1,000,000 on suits purchased at a Geneva boutique, in addition to buying more than 72 pairs of gaudy shoes in unusual colours. Although the suits were never shown to the public, the shoes, which were stored in a warehouse, were photographed by national newspapers. Chiluba never disputed ownership of either the suits or the shoes.

Even if we accept the argument that the former president was entitled to be clothed by the state, the excess shown by President Chiluba must bring into question both his sense of judgement and his values. At the time when the president spent so much money on his personal clothing, more than 70 per cent of the population was living on a dollar a day or less.

Also, the ease with which the president was able to misuse state funds and avoid any kind of enquiry about his spending habits until after he had left office, reveals deficiencies in Zambia's political culture and constitution.

But unethical behaviour does not always translate into punishable criminal conduct. Two years after the London judgement, the Chiluba criminal case in Zambia came to an end. In August 2009, the former president was acquitted of all charges of theft. The presiding magistrate Jones Chinyama found that the prosecution had failed to prove that the money taken out of the Zamtrop account had belonged to the state. In the court of public opinion however Chiluba continued to be guilty, a verdict that guarantees corruption a central place in the former president's legacy.

Mwanawasa's broom

By the time President Chiluba left office, the ruling MMD party had lost most of its shine and there was concern that it might in fact lose the election of late 2001. Two factors were responsible for the ruling party's relative unpopularity. The first was the perceived corruption, and the second was Mr. Chiluba's unwise, clumsy, and ultimately unsuccessful attempt to go for an unconstitutional third term in office.

The December 2001 elections proved to be controversial, with allegations of electoral malpractice amounting to rigging. The public had great difficulty accepting the results which now propelled Chiluba's chosen successor, Levy Mwanawasa, into the presidency. The results were however eventually confirmed by the Supreme

Court, whose decision did nothing to satisfy those who believed the election had been rigged.

Nevertheless the Zambian electorate's punishment of the ruling Movement for Multi-party Democracy was real and severe. Levy Patrick Mwanawasa, the presidential candidate, scraped through with less than 30 per cent of the vote, with his nearest rival, the charming former Anglo American Corporation executive, Anderson Mazoka, taking 27 per cent. In contrast, the MMD presidential candidate in 1991 had secured more than 80 per cent of the vote, with the nearest rival obtaining a mere 18 per cent.

In addition to taking the presidency only by a thin margin in 2001, the MMD saw its proportion of parliamentary seats slashed from 61 per cent to just under 50 per cent, with Mazoka's UPND taking 33 per cent, the Forum for Democracy and Development (FDD) 9 per cent and the United National Independence Party (UNIP) 8 per cent.

Mwanawasa spent the immediate post election period co-opting key members of the opposition into government, although he avoided entering into a formal coalition with other parties. Having thus secured his political base in the legislature, Mwanawasa now turned to addressing his perceived illegitimacy and lack of authority resulting from the narrow victory at the polls.

Mwanawasa needed to do something to divert attention from the legitimacy question and to separate himself from Frederick Chiluba, the political benefactor who had hand picked him as presidential candidate. The new president thus placed the fight against corruption at the centre of his programme. He quickly arranged for President Chiluba's immunity from prosecution to be lifted by parliament. It did not take long after that before charges were laid against Chiluba and other members of the previous MMD government.

Mwanawasa's new broom continued to sweep the government and led to the dismissal of the Vice-President and the Finance Minister who were also loosely accused of corruption, but never charged with the crime. The failure to charge the two senior officials was perhaps an early indication that Mwanawasa's style of fighting corruption would involve quick allegations but not necessarily judicial substantiation of these allegations. It also soon became clear that prosecutions would be selective.

The Task Force on Corruption

In July 2002, some six months after winning the presidential election, President Levy Mwanawasa set up the Task Force on Economic Plunder. The new body, aimed at investigating and prosecuting cases of corruption during the Chiluba era, consisted of officers from the Zambia Police Service, the Drug Enforcement Commission (DEC), the Zambia Security Intelligence Service, and the Anti Corruption Commission.

Thus the director general of the ACC joined the inspector general of police and the commissioner of the DEC as a member of the task force.

The fact that the Task Force was going to be limited in its mandate to suspected cases of corruption between 1991 and 2001 was cause for concern as high level corruption in Zambia has its roots in the one party era and has continued after the end of the Chiluba era. Surely the people of Zambia are entitled to know about corrupt acts that took place before Mr. Chiluba came to power, as they are entitled to reassurance that corruption will not occur in the future.

For this reason the establishment of the Task Force was received with mixed feelings. Most observers of the Zambian political scene questioned the necessity of the Task Force given that Zambia already had a number of investigatory and prosecuting institutions to fight corruption and money laundering. Dr Kaoma Kenneth Mwenda, the Washington based Zambian academic, appears to subscribe to this view. He argues in his book *Legal Aspects of Combating Corruption: the Case of Zambia* that the Task Force in fact usurps the statutory powers and functions of corruption fighting institutions already in existence. According to Dr Mwenda, the Zambian Government should have used its energy and resources to instead strengthen the institutional capacity of the existing agencies and avoided expenditure of the huge amounts of money that the Task Force has incurred for very limited results.

The Task Force has certainly been an expensive enterprise. Ordinarily most prosecutions in Zambia are carried out in magistrates' courts by state employees who need not be lawyers. Prosecutions in higher courts however have to be conducted by state advocates who are lawyers. Depending upon seniority, state advocates earn between US$1,200 and US$2,000 per month. The Task

Force however did not use state advocates in the prosecution of cases. Instead it hired lawyers from private law firms; paying quite hefty retainers in the process. According to the Office of the Vice President, by 2007 the four private sector lawyers prosecuting cases on behalf of the Task Force were receiving a retainer of US$20,000 per month. This was at a time when a young doctor who had spent seven years to qualify, earned, at most, US$500 per month.

In addition to this, four international private prosecutors were paid US$56,450, US$215,443, US$2.7 million and nearly 2.7 million British Pounds, respectively. Furthermore other Zambian law firms were paid US$1,765,280.

These payments may have been justified had a convincing case been made that the lawyers hired to prosecute Task Force matters had special qualifications which were wanting within Government. No such case has ever been made however. As Dr Mwenda has put it:

> There is no convincing evidence to suggest that some of the lawyers contracted by the Zambian Government to prosecute cases for the Task Force have exceptional technical skills in areas pertaining to the fight against corruption or that the concerned individuals are established experts in the field of anti corruption.

On the contrary the evidence suggests that the lawyers engaged by the Task Force had no exceptional skills to justify the kind of money that has been spent on them. The results of the prosecutions also tend to suggest this, with most of the accused being acquitted.

Perhaps the results would have been different had the lawyers prosecuting cases on behalf of the Task Force been selected on merit after a competitive bid process. As desirable as the bid process would have been however, it may not have been enough to give the Task Force constitutional and legal legitimacy.

Section 5 of the 1996 Anti Corruption Commission Act is categorical that the ACC *"shall not, in the performance of its duties, be subject to the direction or control of any person or authority"*. And yet a large part of the Task Force's work consisted of giving direction to the ACC and the DEC. It may be that in future people who have been convicted by the Task Force will bring civil actions designed to show that their convictions were illegal on the ground that they were prosecuted by an illegally constituted body. That argument may or may not succeed. What is clear at the moment is that few see the Task Force as legitimate and capable of delivering justice as envisaged by the Zambian constitution.

In January 2009, Aaron Chungu, whose corruption case was being prosecuted by the Task Force, held a press conference at which he claimed collusion between the Task Force and the judiciary. He also made reference to a memorandum of understanding allegedly entered into between some foreign countries that provide development assistance to Zambia and the Zambian judiciary. According to Chungu, the memorandum of understanding reads in part:

> The successful prosecution of these cases will depend to a large extent on the integrity and competence of the magistrates assigned to handle cases. Whilst the Task Force has no direct influence over the magistrates to individual cases, it will be beneficial to have a few magistrates designated to handle all the cases brought by the Task Force. The Deputy Director of Prosecutions should as far as possible maintain contact with the judiciary on behalf of the Task Force, acting all times within the limits of appreciable behaviour and ethical conduct expected of the legal advisers on behalf of the parties to litigation.

If this memorandum does indeed exist, it must be worrisome to all who believe in fair trials and justice under the Zambian constitution. It would be highly inappropriate for the Task Force as the prosecuting agency to establish an intimate relationship with presiding magistrates at the expense of accused people. It is an established principle of the law that a party to proceedings cannot communicate with the presiding magistrate about the case in the absence of the other party. Doing so would deprive the judicial process of transparency and encourage the very corruption the Task Force purported to fight.

The Cost of Mismanagement

All three republics have been characterized by incompetence and mismanagement, to the detriment of the Zambian people.

While it may be impossible to give the exact amount of money that has been dishonestly taken from the public treasury, it is nonetheless certain that large sums of public money have been misappropriated for as long as the Zambian republic has existed.

The euphoria of independence during the first republic proved greater than demands for probity, which was ironical given the existence of relatively independent institutions that were actually capable of holding the government to account at that time.

The second republic was of course opaque, with the majority of citizens excluded from participation in what the rulers of the day described as 'participatory democracy'. The very structures of the One Party State encouraged waste and inefficiency. Despite the passing of a special law to combat corruption, it was always understood within the ruling elite that corruption would only be punishable when the leadership sanctioned the punishment. The corollary was that corruption could flourish as long as the leadership benefited from or approved of it.

The third republic increased vastly freedom of the press and freedom of expression which led to greater appreciation by the public of the impact of waste and mismanagement of public money on society. A freer debate on corruption also made it easier to detect instances of mismanagement. President Mwanawasa also provided political leadership in the fight against corruption. This was the first time in the country's history that such leadership had been provided. Unfortunately, this did not prevent mismanagement and misappropriation of public money during the Mwanawasa era. Indeed the extent of misappropriation increased under Zambia's third president. Whereas, in 2002, shortly after Mwanawasa's election, only three per cent of Lusaka residents surveyed by Transparency International Zambia believed that corruption was increasing, in a follow-up survey in 2004, this figure had risen to 28 per cent, indicating that corruption was now perceived to be more widespread than it had previously been.

Furthermore, a 2004 study by the National Integrity System found that President Mwanawasa did not address the issue of corruption in his government with the same vigour as he did with respect to suspected corrupt officials who had served in the Chiluba administration.

The best documented evidence of this discrimination came on September 23, 2003, when the Supreme Court delivered its final judgements on two cases outstanding from the 2001 presidential and general elections. The first case involved the veteran journalist and politician Sikota Wina who argued that his ruling party opponent had engaged in electoral malpractice.

The court upheld Mr Wina's complaints and found that there had indeed been malpractice in the conduct of the election in the Mulobezi constituency and that this misconduct had been detrimental to Mr Wina and his opposition United Party for National Development.

Their lordships further ruled that Michael Mabenga, the ruling party candidate, had broken the law when he used government money and vehicles to further his political interests while campaigning for the Mulobezi seat in Western Province. Although this was a civil matter, the judges also took the opportunity to recommend 'appropriate action' by the authorities on the misuse by Mr Mabenga of $6,000 earmarked for the Mulobezi constituency. In the court's view, Mr Mabenga's actions amounted to theft.

The second judgement related to the election in Mpika Central constituency which the court also ruled had not been won fairly.

Despite the ruling and thinly veiled recommendation that Mr Mabenga be charged with theft, President Mwanawasa's government took no action against the erring politician. Indeed Mr Mabenga went on to serve as chairman of the ruling MMD. The lack of action made many in Zambia question the fairness of the fight against corruption. Many continue to believe that luck (or lack thereof) determines who gets prosecuted for corruption in Zambia.

Dr Mwenda makes the point even more strongly. He states on page 44 of *Legal Aspects of Combating Corruption:*

> To a large extent, the crusade to prosecute individuals suspected of having committed offences of corrupt practices is being done on a politically selective basis, arresting and prosecuting only a few sacrificial lambs. The low number of prosecutions faced by corrupt politicians is being done mainly for window dressing purposes, as a political campaign by the State, to win more donor support and funding under the pretext that the State is serious about fighting corruption. A good number of corrupt politicians have retained their status as 'sacred cows' [that] should not be touched by the fight against corruption.

The reader will recall that the accused person Aaron Chungu also made reference to connivance between the Task Force on Corruption and the donor community. Furthermore the incentive to prosecute as many people as possible is quite high given the ample monetary rewards for those fortunate enough to be chosen as prosecutors on behalf of the Task Force, a fact that encouraged spurious prosecutions.

Thus far there has been no comprehensive, systematic and fair programme to fight corruption in Zambia. There have always been 'sacred cows' immune from prosecution. This approach has guaranteed continued mismanagement of public funds.

Although the exact amount of misappropriated money may not be known, Transparency International Zambia has estimated that US$70,000,000 is lost through misappropriation and mismanagement every year. To appreciate the full impact of this on Zambia, it is helpful to examine the uses to which the misappropriated money could be put.

Cameron Sinclair, the London-born executive director of Architecture for Humanity, has become a visible advocate of design for the poorer parts of the world, concentrating his laudable efforts on the design of such things as simple durable shelters and clinics. His alternative approach to architecture is well reflected in the title of a lecture he gave a few years ago, "Design like You Give a Damn."

According to Sinclair who has worked with the Africa Centre for Health and Population Studies in South Africa, constructing a basic clinic capable of reaching 10,000 patients could be done for a cost of $16,000 to $20,000. A fully equipped model would cost $200,000 to build and operate for a year, serving many more people than the basic clinic's 10,000.

Sinclair's figures, and other evidence, give us a good idea of the cost of corruption in Zambia. Even if we assume that the cost of constructing a basic clinic in Zambia would be on the higher end of the Sinclair scale, we must conclude that the $70,000,000 misappropriated or mismanaged every year in Zambia represents 3,500 clinics or 388 new clinics in each of Zambia's nine provinces. In terms of health services delivery potential, the misappropriated money would be more than enough for the provision of basic medical services to 35,000,000 people.

But Zambia's population, at 12 million, would not justify spending the entire sum misappropriated each year on basic clinics. Zambia would have a number of choices, one of which would be to build 1,000 basic clinics and spend $20,000,000 of the money, or build a new fully equipped clinic in each one of the country's 73 districts at a total cost of $14,600,000.

Either way there would be money left over for other projects. If Zambia built fully equipped clinics in each district, there would be $55.4 million left over. That amount would be enough to build one school equivalent to the prestigious Oprah Winfrey Leadership Academy for Girls in South Africa which cost $40 million. But according to Lynn Cole, the head of the Illinois-based Non Governmental Organisation RISE International, a school can actually be built for as little as $12,000

Cole has relevant experience from Angola of building schools on the cheap. Her Angolan schools saw the residents of affected communities do the actual construction. RISE International provided the financing. Groups associated with Illinois high schools like New Trier, Wheeling and West Chicago, as well as churches raised the bulk of the $1.3 million needed to build 150 schools.

On that basis Zambia could build two new schools in each one of the 73 districts at a total cost of $1,687,200. But schools are more than physical buildings; they need teachers and pupils.

The not for profit American organisation Cecily's Fund trains former orphans to become teachers in Zambia, enabling them to contribute toward the education of a whole new generation of children. For $60 per month, Cecily's Fund guarantees tuition fees and all living expenses for student teachers. In addition to working with local Zambian partner organizations to enable orphans and vulnerable children attend primary and secondary school, Cecily's Fund also trains 40 to 50 graduates each year as health educators.

It is estimated that in 2008 there were 800,000 Zambian children who could not attend formal education because they lived too far from a school or came from families that were too poor to finance even a modest education. Assuming a one-year intensive teacher training course, 40,000 teachers could be trained under the Cecily's Fund plan to teach classes of 20 children each at a cost of $28,000,000. For that additional money Zambia would guarantee an education to every single child.

So, with the money misappropriated each year Zambia could build a fully equipped clinic and two new schools in each of Zambia's 73 districts, in addition to training teachers to provide an education to the 800,000 children who do not currently attend school. After all this, there would still be $25,713,000 left over. Perhaps this money could be used to bolster the pay of medical workers and teachers.

A 2006 study by David Lusale, a Senior Lecturer in Reproductive Health at Chainama College of Health Sciences in the Zambian capital, Lusaka, shows that on average nurses receive a monthly salary of US$229. Clinical officers are remunerated at the monthly rate US$299. These salary rates are low not only when compared to the international norm but also domestically in the context of monthly food requirements estimated in the range of US$350 for a family of six.

According to Lusale, "These low salaries are an important factor driving nurses and clinical officers to 'breaking point' and the decision to migrate from the governmental sector and search for new jobs that could pay them a better living wage." Teachers (who earn about $100 a month) and doctors (who are paid about $500 per month) are not much better remunerated than nurses and all three professions necessarily take a pay cut when the Zambian currency depreciates, as is the case at the time of writing. The members of these critical professions must be guaranteed a living wage at all times.

The Cumulative Cost of Corruption

What we have looked at represents the cost of financial mismanagement and other forms of corruption in one year. Financial mismanagement is however ongoing. This means that the actual amount of money misappropriated grows with time as the impact of the corruption becomes exponential and pervasive. More and more people are affected as the impact of financial mismanagement is felt.

According to Transparency International Zambia (TIZ), the equivalent of US$1,392,800,000 was "misappropriated, stolen or grossly mismanaged" from 1984 to 2004. This represents almost half the amount required to finance Zambia's 15 trillion Kwacha budget for 2009. The actual amount misappropriated is, according to TIZ probably much larger than this. The difficulty of calculating the exact amount of money misused is compounded by systemic weaknesses in government accounting systems. Indeed government practices themselves exacerbate waste, if not encourage outright theft.

For example, the practice in Zambia is that a civil servant invited to attend a meeting at another government ministry will be paid an attendance allowance. Allowances are extremely important to Zambian civil servants as they often exceed the pay (calculated on a daily basis) that public servants ordinarily receive. Seminars and workshops that take place at resorts outside the capital are particularly popular. A civil servant (or indeed politician) attending one of these seminars will be entitled to a sum of money for telephone use, full reimbursement of hotel bills, in addition to meal allowance, even when the hotel bill includes the cost of food consumed in the hotel.

These abuses are such an established feature of public service practice in Zambia that they rarely attract the attention of the auditor general whose principal function is to track the expenditure of public money by the government. Even excluding these practices however, cases of abuse highlighted by the auditor general demonstrate how widespread corruption is and how lax the Government is in making wrongdoers accountable, unless of course they happen to be political enemies.

Three examples from a publication by TIZ, *Show Me the Money,* illustrate the point.

In the Kabwe Passport Office case, cashiers in the capital of Zambia's central province stole more than US$5000 and failed to account for another US$15,800. As far as is known the cashiers were never charged, even though their misappropriation of funds was well known and documented in the auditor general's report for 2004.

The second example is the PACRO case involving staffers at the Patents and Companies Registration Office which is supervised by the Ministry of Commerce, Trade and Industry. The staffers in question took advantage of weaknesses in internal control systems to loot an undisclosed sum of money between 1999 and 2002. Mr Richard Chizyuka, the Permanent Secretary and therefore controlling officer, admitted that during the period under review, his ministry did not supervise PACRO. No disciplinary action appears to have been taken against Mr Chizyuka, and neither were the perpetrators of the theft prosecuted. Later, in the course of a civil trial in London resulting from alleged corrupt practices by former president Frederick Chiluba, Mr

Chizyuka was to admit to financial impropriety with the mitigating plea that he was "not a habitual bribe taker"!

The last example comes from Solwezi where the municipal council underwent a forensic audit which revealed huge financial irregularities. The auditor's report showed misuse of the US$33,600 given to the council as a grant. The condition of the grant was that 70 per cent of the money should be spent on social services. Instead the council used 75 per cent of the money for salaries, allowances for councillors and mobile telephones for chief officers. Only 25 per cent went toward social services. An even more disturbing aspect of the report was the finding that US$ 86,700 meant for retirees, retrenched workers and families of deceased employees had been misappropriated by the town clerk and senior officers who were said to have paid themselves from council accounts without authority. Again, no charges appear to have been brought against the town clerk and his senior officers.

In late 2008 and early 2009 however, the Solwezi Municipal Council levied rates in the amount of US$1,000,000 against an international mining company in violation of that company's agreement with the Zambian Government that no taxes other than the ones contained in the Development Agreement would be paid by the company. The council went so far as to order seizure of the mining company's assets and succeeded in disrupting operations at the mine, all in the name of raising funds to finance social services in Solwezi.

There are examples of mismanagement from every era in Zambian history suggesting that the country has been badly governed since its inception as a modern state. Although political emancipation in 1964 ended colonial rule and opened up economic opportunities for more people, little attention was paid to the individual rights of these people. Equally there was no commitment to the creation of a transparent and democratic system of government that rewarded those who worked hard and played by the rules.

During Zambia's early years as an independent republic these challenges were masked by the euphoria of recent emancipation and the novelty of having an indigenous government in power.

The challenges were by no means insurmountable. Had the country continued as a democracy, there would have been, in due course, more demands for better government. Unfortunately the advent of the one party state undermined the evolution of a transparent and accountable democracy, and instead provided the perfect setting for mismanagement and dictatorship. There was no longer a leader of the opposition to worry about, and the auditor general was totally under the influence of the ruling party.

The reintroduction of democracy in 1991 provided some hope in the early stages but it soon became clear that the one party culture had survived democratisation. The institutional weaknesses that had allowed corruption to enter Zambian political life on a large scale now enabled President Chiluba's excesses to go unchallenged. It was going to take firm political leadership to banish corruption and mismanagement from the Zambian political scene.

The presidency of Levy Patrick Mwanawasa offered such political leadership. Sadly his campaign against misappropriation of public money was to be selective. Only opponents of the regime or other people not considered members of the political elite were at risk of prosecution. The Shamabanse principle was alive and well, and inadvertently given official recognition when President Mwanawasa decided to confer posthumously the Order of the Eagle of Zambia, Second Division on Henry Shamabanse, making one of the pioneers of official corruption an official hero.

If the politicians have been casual in the fight against corruption, the judiciary too has its share of the blame. The Zambian judicial system is notoriously slow in resolving cases. President Chiluba, for example, was the subject of judicial and quasi judicial proceedings for seven years before his trial was finally concluded in 2009.

The slowness of the judiciary has undermined the fight against corruption as citizens have concluded from the delay in successfully prosecuting accused people, that perhaps the prosecutions were unjustified and politically motivated. The Task Force did not help matters in this regard. Its very existence was on shaky constitutional ground and its practices appeared to support the view that prosecutions were selectively done. The credibility of these prosecutions was further undermined by the close relationship that the Task Force is perceived to have with the judiciary. When eventually President Banda abolished the Task Force there was only token resistance to the move.

Good governance is the process by which public institutions conduct public affairs, manage public resources and guarantee the realization of human rights in a confidence inspiring way that is free of abuse and corruption, and with due regard for the rule of law. The internationally accepted test of "good governance" is the degree to which the model of government delivers on the promise of human rights and provides opportunities for true enjoyment of civil, cultural, economic, political and social rights. The former United Nations Commission on Human Rights posed the following question in determining the existence of good governance: 'Are the institutions of governance effectively guaranteeing the right to health, adequate housing, sufficient food, quality education, fair justice and personal security?' In Zambia's case the answer must be in the negative for now.

CHAPTER 4

A Culture of Neglect

When Kenneth Kaunda promised 'an egg a day for every Zambian' during the campaign for independence, he meant well, and may even have believed that he could actually deliver on the promise. What he may not have realised however was that, this promise, together with other wilder claims of the time, such as free high quality health care and education for every Zambian, were the psychological preparation for a culture of dependency and unreasonable expectation.

Today there is a palpable shortage of personal responsibility in Zambia. Few nationals feel a sense of personal responsibility for their well being and the collective health of their community; abdicating the responsibility of caring for themselves and their families to the state. Equally, not enough Zambians have developed a sense of proprietorship over public assets and hence are able to play the necessary custodial role with respect to public money. The neglect evident in both the personal and communal lives of Zambians coupled with the country's dependency on government and the international community is both excessive and embarrassing.

This culture has of course facilitated corruption as society has largely given up its role as overseer of pubic spending. Politicians and other officials have thus had a freer hand in misappropriating public funds. The result of corruption and suppression of personal initiative is that Zambia, a country with arguably the most placid people in world, an abundance of water and other natural resources, not to mention an agreeable climate and fertile land, is now one of the poorest countries in the world. Given all its advantages, the country has no business being poor. As the late Gwen Konie, Zambia's first female graduate, observed, 'Zambia is a rich country that is poorly managed.'

The country is indeed poorly managed.

The absence of an effective infrastructure, for example, has resulted in small scale farmers in some parts of the country being unable to market their produce, and letting much of that produce go to waste, even in times of food shortages elsewhere in the country. Poor planning and an official lack of confidence in individual Zambians has led to large numbers of skilled nationals being unemployed, at the same time as the Government has turned to foreign donors to fill the 'skills gap'. In the circumstances it is perhaps not surprising that most Zambians now consider themselves fortunate when they 'survive'; believing success to be out of reach.

With such limited ambition and goals, as well as an absence of effective support from the Government, a culture of neglect (and even lethargy) has developed in the general population. The unemployed feel helpless and have no individual standards to speak of; but even persons in full time employment show little pride in their work. This is certainly the case in the public sector. There is no shortage of examples of public servants who simply cannot be bothered to do a better job. There was for example, the television news reader who had the most unfortunate pronunciation for the phrase, Shiite Muslim. The news reader or the producer of the programme could have ascertained the correct pronunciation from anyone of the Islamic missions in Lusaka, but no one bothered. That same national broadcaster spent tens of thousands of dollars on a brand new four wheel drive vehicle for the chief executive officer, but was at the same time unable to keep the public toilets on the premises clean and usable.

There is any number of customer service personnel at public institutions who make it clear that they prefer to talk to friends over the phone, than quickly serve members of the public in need of urgent help at the counter.

There are of course public servants who strive to do their best despite a lack of encouragement. In July 2008 I visited the Livingstone Railway Museum and was extremely impressed with the guide's knowledge of the trains he shows off to the public. He clearly loves his job. Most of his colleagues were equally enthusiastic about their jobs.

Unfortunately the museum is in such a state of disrepair and so poorly advertised that this guide and his colleagues have little opportunity to perform the duties they are so passionate about.

There are thus in Zambia failings at both the institutional and individual levels which allow the insouciance of politicians and other government officials to go largely unchallenged by the citizenry. While the railway museum guide would dearly love to serve his country well, this feeling is not shared by many senior public officials.

Serving One's country

The general absence of personal responsibility and the failure of many citizens to take a proprietary interest in public property are noticeable not only among less educated Zambians but also among supposedly informed Zambians fortunate enough to work in government. The evidence is that very few in this privileged class make it their business to be constantly on the look out for opportunities beneficial to their country.

In 1995 I was living in Ottawa where the Zambian High Commission to Canada was located. It was never obvious to me what the benefit to Zambia of the mission was, and it was this office I had in mind when that year I suggested during a television interview that now that the cold war had ended Zambia should take a different view of diplomatic representation. Specifically, I suggested that the country should look at every embassy as an investment expected to yield a return. In the case of Ottawa the mission's main preoccupation had to be drumming up business for Zambia in Canada. For example, Zambia could adopt a strategy aimed at attracting a modest 10 per cent of Canadian dollars spent on tourism each year. Given that Canadians were at that time spending $13 billion on travel to warmer climates during their winter, this strategy, if successful, would yield an income of $1.3 billion for Zambia- an amount greater than the country was earning from its principal export of copper at the time. I also thought there should be a more aggressive engagement of the Canadian Diaspora.

An opportunity to collaborate with the Ottawa mission had in fact arisen about a year earlier. I had heard that the University of Zambia was experiencing a critical shortage of books in science subjects. My immediate thought was that I might be able to raise enough money buy books for the students at home. It then occurred to me that there might be a supply of second hand books with reasonably current scientific information that I could tap into. I saw my main task as identifying the source of the books and collecting the texts. I was confident that if I got these books to one location in Ottawa, the Zambian mission would do the rest. At that point all that would be required was transportation of the material to a port for onward shipment to Lusaka.

Identifying the source of books turned out to be easier than I had anticipated. The church where my family and I worshipped was located in Orleans, Ontario, a community with a significant number of military personnel with a science background.

One Sunday I announced to the congregation that I was interested in science books for the University of Zambia. I stipulated that I would welcome any books in Mathematics, Physics, Chemistry, Biology, Computer Science, or General Science, as long as these books were no older than three years. I could see right away that the congregation was keen to help. A number of the congregants spoke to me after the service to make sure that they understood what the requirements were.

Not only was the message perfectly understood, the response was almost immediate and certainly overwhelming. Within a fortnight, the Queenswood United Church had collected enough books to fill the spare office, which measured roughly 100 square feet, from floor to ceiling. The congregation made it clear however that they would be happy to collect even more books.

I was elated with the response to the needs of a university in a far away land that many congregants could not even pinpoint on a map. I was sure Zambia's high commissioner to Canada would be even more pleased than I was. I would call him as soon as possible and make an appointment to see him.

I was going to deliver the news in person, not over the phone; I wanted the pleasure of seeing his face when I told him what the good men and women of Queenswood United Church had done.

When the time to see His Excellency the High Commissioner for the Republic of Zambia came, I was confident that within weeks the science section of the University of Zambia library would be rich beyond expectation.

It was not to be. His Excellency received me well enough but also made it clear he was not prepared to invest his time in something that was not going to work. He opined that even if he did find a way of getting the books to Lusaka, there was no guarantee that they could be transported from the point of landing to the University. In any event who was going to pay for the transportation of the books, he asked.

I was completely taken aback by the envoy's reaction. He made absolutely no effort to think of ways of getting the badly needed material to Zambia. But I could do nothing further. The High Commissioner's mind was made up. And so I left the Zambian mission in a state of dejection, questioning the value of diplomats in the post cold war world.

It was just as well that my next meeting with an envoy was a few days later with Fadhil Mbaga, the Tanzanian diplomat whose company I always enjoyed. Mr Mbaga was a mild mannered and unassuming diplomat who kept himself extremely well informed. Perhaps because of this he had almost miraculously managed to persuade the Canadian government to abandon its policy of drastically reducing economic aid to Tanzania.

Fadhil Mbaga had sought my opinion on the matter, hoping that I would have some useful insight as a former consultant in international development. In fact the meeting I was now looking forward to with Mr. Mbaga was about possible strategies he might adopt in his negotiations with the Canadians.

The meeting took place in the High Commission library because High Commissioner Mbaga's office was being painted at that time.

We had concluded our discussions and were now enjoying a cup of Tanzanian tea when I asked Mr. Mbaga about the "book situation" at the University of Dar Es Salaam. His response was that in general the university was well equipped but there was a shortage of science books. Of course I could not resist asking if, in the event of science books being available, his mission would be able to transport the consignment to Tanzania. To this day I remember vividly Mbaga's reaction. He leant forward and said, "My brother, if that happened, I would do whatever it took to get the books home."

The gloom was lifting. Zambia may not benefit from my efforts, but a neighbouring country with a conscientious high commissioner, would. I told High Commissioner Mbaga that on my return from Toronto I would introduce him to Queenswood United Church so that he could arrange to collect the books from Orleans and store them on High Commission premises until they could be transported to Tanzania. It would take at least a week for me to speak to Queenswood United Church because I would be out of town for five days. In those days I worked in Toronto but lived in Ottawa.

When I left Mbaga's office, I was certain he did not believe it really could be that easy to source books for Tanzania's oldest university. I would surprise him.

I returned from Toronto and discovered that it was me who was to be surprised. I called the church to alert them to a visit I would be making with the Tanzanians in connection with the books. There was hesitation at the other end and then this response: "They have already been here and taken the books!"

Although I was delighted by the news I was curious as to why Mr. Mbaga had not forewarned me. When I called him later, the envoy explained that he could not wait for my return from Toronto because he had heard that there was a half empty container going to Dar Es Salaam from a Canadian port and he wanted to seize the opportunity to transport his books on this container. The High Commissioner had spent the bulk of his time in the last few days negotiating with the owners of the container and arranging for the consignment of books to be delivered to port. Once again Fadhil Mbaga had lived up to his reputation as an effective operator.

Mbaga had served his country well. The Zambian High Commissioner had not. Why had the Zambian envoy allowed this opportunity to go unexploited? Sadly the Zambian envoy had not behaved atypically. I was not the only member of the Diaspora to be let down in this way by Zambian officialdom.

Dr Wyndioto Frank Chisela is a world class nuclear physicist who practices medical physics. He is now based in the American state of Georgia, after stints in Ontario Canada, New York State, as well as Wisconsin.

In 2006 Dr Chisela was given an appointment to see President Levy Mwanawasa and the then first lady, Maureen, while the couple was visiting Washington DC. At that time, Dr Chisela lived in upstate New York and was therefore obliged to purchase a plane ticket to Washington DC in order to make the appointment. The primary purpose of the meeting was to present to the first couple an initiative he was working on. That initiative would result in the donation of American hospital equipment to Zambian hospitals.

Dr Chisela is a medical physicist professional with special competence in cancer radiation therapy. At that time he had worked in this field for some fifteen years, holding senior positions both in Canada and the USA.

The meeting went well with the first couple being attentive and interested in all issues raised by Chisela including economic problems facing Zambia and the shortage of qualified personnel to manage Zambian institutions. The main purpose of the meeting however, was to inform the first couple about the hospital equipment initiative.

Dr Chisela told the president and Mrs Mwanawasa about offers he had received from his own hospital and other hospitals in the area, for used hospital beds that were available for donation. The hospitals were prepared to donate the equipment to any organization able to store and subsequently transport the equipment to its final destination.

Dr Chisela had done a huge amount of homework to ensure that the equipment got to Zambia. Amongst other things he had contacted the Rotary Club asking them for information regarding shipment of such equipment to his homeland. He had chosen the Rotary Club after learning that one of their chapters in his residential neighbourhood had just completed a shipment of similar equipment to Zambia's neighbour, Zimbabwe. The Rotary Club had indicated a willingness to use its contacts in Zambia to act as a recipient on behalf of the country's health ministry.

Not unnaturally, His Excellency the President (as Mwanawasa was routinely referred to) was extremely enthusiastic. The first lady too shared this enthusiasm. The couple expressed their willingness to do whatever was necessary to expedite the Chisela initiative. To that end Dr Chisela was introduced to the Zambian Ambassador who was directed to work closely with the medical physicist so that the task at hand could be completed as soon as possible. The ambassador wasted no time that evening to collect information pertaining to the quality, quantity, and location of the beds. The ambassador also promised to meet Dr Chisela again later that month to finalize the plans of how and when to move this equipment from the donor hospitals to its eventual destination in Zambia.

Dr Chisela was elated after the meeting; he had an opportunity to finally do something for sick people in his country. He went home and immediately started working with his contacts, assuring them that the Zambian embassy in Washington DC would participate in the coordination of the project.

Unfortunately, the ambassador never contacted Dr Chisela after the meeting in Washington. Chisela called the envoy on a number of occasions but never heard back. In the end, the medical physicist had no option but to walk away from the project "and [withdraw] all my bids as a recipient for donated hospital equipment". Dr Chisela described the episode as "a great disappointment".

The former envoys to Ottawa and Washington make the case for a new approach in managing Zambian diplomatic representation, and perhaps the very process by which envoys are selected. Both diplomats missed the opportunity to serve their country. In both cases the substantive work had been done by a member of the Diaspora. All that was asked of the envoys was to facilitate transportation. This was not an impossible task, as High Commissioner Mbaga of Tanzania so easily demonstrated. The Zambian envoys failed to listen to their conscience. One of them in fact disregarded specific direction from his head of state. This is but one step away from disregarding the country's laws.

A Casual View of the Law

The reader will not be surprised that the culture of neglect has led to disregard of laws and regulations and the abandonment of the culture of personal responsibility and enterprise widely evident in Zambia until the mid 1970s. The case of Joseph Sanken, whom we met earlier, is a case in point. The reader will recall that Mr Sanken was a peasant farmer detained on suspicion of belonging to a terrorist organisation. Preliminary investigations suggested that Sanken had no connection to the terrorist organisation. Because of this, he was issued with a pre signed Revocation of Detention Order. But someone forgot to tell Joseph he was free to go. He waited at the police station where he was held until all detainees were transferred to prisons. When he arrived at Mpima State Prison, the authorities there were shown Joseph's original detention order, and on that basis admitted him as a political prisoner. Joseph Sanken spent some four years as a political prisoner at Mpima State Prison. He was never charged with any offence and, of course, never tried.

Sadly, Joseph Sanken was not the only person to be treated in such a cavalier fashion. Protection of human rights and adherence to laws and regulations were not always a paramount consideration in the actions of the state. This attitude led government officials often to take unreasonable and unconscionable risks in the daily execution of their duties.

On October 20, 1981, I was a political prisoner at Mpima State Prison. I was told by the prison authorities to pack my bags in preparation for the journey to Lusaka where my petition for torture and unlawful imprisonment against the state was due to be heard the following day. We had known about the case for almost two weeks but the authorities chose to make travel arrangements at the last minute. As a political prisoner, I was provided the usual armed police escort for the trip between Mpima and the capital. The vehicle used on this occasion was the Aro, a Romanian made Jeep-like contraption whose performance and reliability could not have been further from the American creation.

We left Mpima at about 5:20 pm, more than two hours after I had been told to get ready. The distance between Kabwe and Lusaka is about 144 kilometres and is normally covered in 90 minutes by prudent drivers. Had we left Mpima on schedule, we would have arrived in Lusaka at 5 pm at the latest, or before dusk.

Instead dusk found us ten minutes' drive outside Kabwe. It was at this point that we discovered the vehicle's lights were not working. The driver, a paramilitary sergeant, seemed to think this was a minor matter and decided to press on with the journey, somehow believing that it would not get any darker. And so we drove on in the increasing darkness until we reached the Ploughman's Arms, a structurally sound but poorly maintained resort. At this point I had made up my mind that it would be grossly unfair to accuse our driver of being a genius, so I made a suggestion that in most other circumstances would have been too obvious to make. I wondered aloud if it might not be useful to check the fuses. I hoped that if the problem lay in a burnt fuse even the Aro would carry a spare and we would use that to restore the lighting system to working order. A burnt fuse was not however the problem as an attendant at the resort's garage confirmed.

I made one more attempt to influence the driver's thinking by opining that it might be useful if we called Lusaka and asked the police for help. At that time of the day, they could reach us in about an hour. The driver felt however that he had a much better idea. We could simply trail another Lusaka bound vehicle, and using that vehicle's lights we would be able to eventually reach Lusaka safely. The sergeant did not apparently consider the possibility of the vehicle being trailed increasing its speed and leaving us behind or even deciding to branch off the main road.

It did not take long before the remarkable lack of foresight in the driver's idea became self evident. We were unable to keep up with the unilaterally appointed guiding vehicle, and were soon plunged into total darkness. It was only then that it dawned on the paramilitary officer that perhaps we should have called Lusaka for help when we had a chance to do so at the Ploughman's Arms. To his credit, the driver now showed some resourcefulness by identifying the nearest police station to where we were. That station was in the farming area of Chisamba. In order to get there we would have to branch off the main road and turn into a gravel road which would have virtually no traffic on it. A more sensible option would have been to get a lift back to the Ploughman's Arms and call the Chisamba Police Station from there. Unfortunately, the driver was bent on driving to Chisamba Station in the lightless Aro. Thus he continued on the main road hoping to miraculously identify signs for Chisamba. Some twenty minutes later our ride became unusually bumpy with a concentrated sound of gravel against the windscreen as well as the brushing sounds of tree branches in full assault on the Aro. Not only had we landed in a ditch, we were also on the wrong side of the road.

This time there was no choice but to seek real help. We were fortunate to flag down a truck, whose driver not only helped us retrieve our vehicle from the ditch but also agreed to guide us to the Emmasdale Police Station on the outskirts of Lusaka where the local officers gave us a Land Rover to continue our journey to the Lusaka Central Prison where I was booked for the night.

Why had we left Kabwe as late as we did? Why did the authorities appear entirely unprepared for my trip to Lusaka when they had in fact known about it for a while. Why did the paramilitary driver take the risk of driving at night without lights? Why did he behave so irresponsibly? Why did he not follow basic traffic regulations and better protect the well being of his passengers?

It is tempting to blame the culture of the second republic for both the driver's lack of initiative and his recklessness. But this behaviour has continued into the third republic. While it is unlikely that today (given the abundance of motor vehicle spare parts) any official would drive a government vehicle at night with no lights, it is not unusual to see drivers of government vehicles violating established road traffic laws and environmental regulations. There is no shortage of government vehicles, for example, with malfunctioning exhaust systems that drive along the busy roads of Lusaka nonchalantly spewing toxic material into the atmosphere. Government drivers do not set a good example to other motorists and because of this there appears now to be a general belief in Zambia that only laws that can conveniently be obeyed at a particular time need in fact be obeyed.

Observing drivers cross the four way stop near Lusaka's St Ignatius Church, is quite instructive in this regard. In general, motorists are unaware of the rules governing behaviour at a four way stop. The basic rule that the fist to arrive at the stop takes precedence is more often ignored than respected. And of course most motorists are totally confused when two vehicles arrive at the same time. In the absence of information, many motorists now treat crossing a four way stop as a game of chance, apparently without regard to the potentially deadly nature of the game.

This tendency is noticeable at virtually all four way stops in Lusaka and other Zambian cities, albeit with less frequency in more affluent areas. Some of the intersections are of course regulated by traffic lights. But even here, there is absolute pandemonium when traffic lights suddenly stop working.

On these occasions motorists seem to be satisfied that they have discharged their responsibility by simply slowing down and blowing the horn. The chaos continues until the police send an officer to the scene to manually direct traffic. It has to be said that the traffic section of the Zambia Police has not been negligent in responding reasonably quickly to these situations in Lusaka.

Even so, the question must be asked: Why has no effort been made to educate the public about four way stop procedures? An even more troubling question is: How did motorists who do not know basic four way stop procedures, obtain their driving licences?

I put the question to officials at the Road Transport and Safety Agency. The people I spoke to were extremely well qualified professionals. They agreed that it would be useful to educate the public about four way stop regulations. We discussed the insertion of advertisements in newspapers on a regular basis as one way of achieving this. That conversation took place more than a year before the time of writing. As far as I know, no such advertisements have been placed in the local press. Crossing four way stops in Zambia continues to be largely a game of chance.

Zoning Laws

Disregard of the law is by no means confined to traffic regulations. Former Zambian residents who left the country in the early 1970s are shocked to see the state of disrepair of many homes and public buildings, when they return. Without exception all local governments in Zambia have been negligent in the area of town planning and property maintenance. Citizens too have tended to disregard their obligations under town planning and zoning laws.

Zambia has reasonably elaborate zoning laws, but these are only applied when it is convenient for the local authority (or an individual in local authority) to do so.

The Copperbelt town of Chingola always prided itself as the cleanest town in Zambia. The entrance to the town consisted (as it still does) of a large roundabout with a well manicured lawn and a concentration of aesthetically pleasing flowers and plants on the edge and in the middle. Until the late 1970s the famous roundabout was surrounded by neatly painted houses, also with manicured lawns. The city streets were broad and well maintained. Every single street was sign posted. This was certainly the case in the low density area which encompasses what North Americans call 'downtown'. But even the high density housing areas had a semblance of order and the houses there more often than not would have a patch of lawn at the front and possibly a small vegetable garden at the back. The main streets in Chiwempala, one of the high density areas, were paved and well maintained. In the early 1970s Town Clerk Tunji Fahm made it a personal mission to ensure that his beloved Chingola was kept clean and well maintained at all times. The Chingola Municipal Council had an entire department dedicated to maintaining roads. Both the low density areas and the high density areas had land reserved for parks. No one could build on these pieces of land.

One such designated park was in what the British colonial government called the second class trading area along Zambezi Road. The road services a strip mall consisting of a butchery, shops, supermarkets, and two lounge bars. There was a park at the southern end of the mall. In the late 1990s the mall's character was entirely ruined not just by the construction of illegal stalls on the eastern side, but also by the allocation of the park to a 'developer' who added insult to injury by constructing a shack that violated the most basic building code. The allocation of land itself was done in violation of the Council's zoning by laws. Why did this happen? Why was the officer responsible for this illegal act not brought to book?

We may not know the answers to these questions but we do know the consequences of the allocation and other similar acts; it is to legitimise the disregard of laws. Not long afterwards the City of Ndola, capital of the Copperbelt Province, allowed a petroleum storage company to build a fuel storage centre along the busy Ndola-Kabwe road, barely a few meters from the main road.

As if this were not enough, the company was also allowed to construct huge tanks (for the storage of flammable liquids) almost directly beneath electric power lines. All this was done in clear violation of zoning and environmental laws. The construction was also remarkably short sighted. It is clear to all that the Ndola-Kabwe highway is ripe for conversion into a dual carriage way, on account of the increased traffic. When that decision is finally taken, the authorities will be unable to proceed with the construction of the additional lanes without first removing the ugly and intrusive structures of the petroleum storage company. The exercise of expanding this important trunk road will be that much harder and more expensive because of the myopic decision to disregard zoning and environmental laws in granting permission to a company to construct oil storage facilities.

In fairness it must be said that the Ndola City Council had apparently resisted the construction of the storage tanks on this site but the petroleum company was partly owned by politically influential people who were able to pressure the council into agreeing to the illegal construction.

The issue with this construction was not just proximity to a busy road; it was also proximity to the power lines. In an attempt to resolve the latter, it was agreed that the Zambia Electricity Supply Company (ZESCO) which owns the power lines would move the lines to a safe distance, on condition that the cost of so doing was borne by the petroleum company. The money was reportedly paid to ZESCO but the power lines were never moved.

Why was this construction allowed to take place despite the obvious dangers? A fire at the company could easily lead to numerous deaths and destruction of a large section of the city.

In 2009, there was another example of gross negligence from ZESCO. It was reported in early June that the rampant growth of water weed near a hydro-electric dam in Zambia had cut the electricity supply, causing widespread blackouts.

ZESCO acknowledged this and said the weed on the Kafue River had restricted the flow of water to the electricity plant, cutting the power supply by a quarter. ZESCO further said it would now be forced to ration power to domestic users and copper mines.

The Zambian government acknowledged that the company had been negligent in allowing the weed to grow right up to the power turbines. In this case, ZESCO ignored procedures that would be considered basic by any power generating company relying on hydro electric power.

It was not the first time that basic procedures had been ignored. In early May 2009 residents of Chinsali District in the Northern Province threatened to take legal action against ZESCO when they lost property as a result of a ZESCO transformer developing a fault and supplying more voltage than normal. The surge in power led to equipment being damaged.

This was not the first time that Chinsali residents had lost property in this way. Similar losses had occurred in 2008. Then, as now, the residents were not compensated for the loss they suffered. The residents were shocked by ZESCO's lack of responsibility especially in light of the fact that the company had been aware for some time that the transformer was faulty.

Chinsali is one of the least developed towns in Zambia but a number of businesspeople there are making an effort to revitalize the local economy. These businesspeople were particularly hit as they lost computers and appliances subjected to abnormally high voltage.

Unfortunate as it was however, the Chinsali episode was mild compared to other acts of ZESCO's negligence which have actually threatened life, in addition to destroying property. In October 2005 Nicholas Chibwaku, a resident of Kafue town, just south of Lusaka, complained that a ZESCO power cable had caused his son's paralysis.

According to Mr Chibwaku, on June 20, 2004, his son John was electrocuted by a live ZESCO cable that had been lying unprotected for more than two months. John was electrocuted after a sugar cane he was carrying came into contact with the loose cable. John suffered severe body burns and was obliged to spend six months in hospital. The Chibwaku family received no compensation and their efforts to sue the electricity company came to nothing.

Any legal action against ZESCO seems doomed to failure. In 2008 a family from the low density housing area of Roma in Lusaka experienced a huge surge in power supply to their home. The effect of the surge was to gut their house and destroy everything in it. Fortunately for the family, the incident occurred during the day and they were able to get out in time. They were not however able to save any of their property. The family was entirely blameless. For this reason it was assumed that ZESCO would be liable to compensate them for the house and belongings lost in the fire. It was not to be. The family's lawyer advised after studying the legislation governing ZESCO that the electricity company had no obligation at all to compensate the innocent victims. Any hope of compensation must lie in negotiations with ZESCO leading to an *ex gratia* payment. The family did not hold its breath; irresponsible companies do not make voluntary offers of compensation. Sadly, in the case of ZESCO, the law appears to protect corporate negligence and irresponsible behaviour. Perhaps the family should have turned its attention to the fire department which not only showed up late, but arrived at the scene of the fire without water!

A year after the Roma house fire ZESCO was in trouble yet again. Moses Mulenga, a resident of another Northern town, Kasama, sued the power company for negligence which allegedly resulted in the death by electrocution of the complainant's relative. Mr Mulenga did not rely on legislation governing the operations of ZESCO but rather on the broader Fatal Accidents Act.

The facts in the Mulenga case were not too dissimilar from the facts in the Chibwaku case.

Bartholomew Mulenga, the victim, was walking home on the evening of November 22, 2006, when he was electrocuted by live wires that had been cut and carelessly placed on the ground near the sub-station serving Mulenga's village. Bartholomew sustained severe electrical burns which were described as "charred right hemi-face, anterior chest wall, fore limbs, lower limbs, peritoneum, intestines, genitalia and pericardium basal wall." The victim subsequently died from the burns. It appears the cables Bartholomew had come in contact with were unsecured. ZESCO's alleged failure to take reasonable care for the safety of unsuspecting members of the public as well as failing to provide security at the site where the live cables lay, was at the centre of the legal claim. At the time of writing the matter has not been judicially determined.

While the irresponsible behaviour of ZESCO is well documented, corporate and institutional irresponsibility is by no means confined to state companies. There are examples of negligence too from both local government as well as central government.

Every town in Zambia has by laws which require buildings to conform to zoning laws and to be maintained. In addition many properties in urban areas are acquired by way of under leases from municipal councils. These under leases often specify that buildings must be painted at reasonable intervals; others require lawns to be manicured.

The City of Ndola, like other older cities and towns in Zambia, has some historic buildings of interest. Government House on Buteko Avenue is an example. The other example is the building on President Avenue that houses a famous pharmacy. Apart from their colonial charm, now quite hidden, the two buildings have one other thing in common - they are both poorly maintained. A coat of paint may not be enough to fully restore these buildings to their former glory but it might be enough to highlight their external aesthetic qualities.

It is clear that enforcing by laws and attending to town planning matters is not a priority for most local authorities in Zambia. Instead the priorities seem to centre on pomp and prestige. This has led to reduced expenditure on services and disproportionate expenditure on emoluments and unproductive activities. With less money being spent on services, more Zambians have found themselves living in unsanitary conditions.

Kanyama Township is an entirely unplanned habitat south of Lusaka. For the most part the area has no running water and exhibits all the characteristics of a slum neglected by officialdom. Since the late 1970s Kanyama has been the victim of flooding in each year that Zambia has had anything resembling above normal rainfall. The first recorded serious deluge occurred around 1978. Times were different then and the country was more responsive to suffering than it is now. Businesspeople and ordinary men and women were joined by the international community in raising money for what came to be known as the Kanyama Disaster Fund. The purpose of the fund was to help accommodate, feed and otherwise help the victims of the disaster.

Since it was clear from the start that the flooding could have been avoided had the Lusaka City Council constructed an appropriate drainage system, the hope was that drainage infrastructure would now be put in place to avoid similar calamities in the future.

Sadly that did not happen. There was no public explanation either of how the huge amount of money raised was used by the local authority. Virtually each rainy season brings deleterious flooding to Kanyama, with the deluge of 1978 proportions being repeated frequently in the recent past. This was certainly the case during the 2009/2010 rainy season which caused widespread flooding.

The *Post* newspaper edition of March 10, 2010 described the flooding as a 'death trap'. The newspaper had reason to do so. At least 12 children in the area were reported to have died in the floods. During the week that *The Post* article was written, the government and the Zambia Red Cross Society relocated over 800 people to the Lusaka Independence Stadium where they were obliged to sleep in tents, use mobile toilets, and prepare food in communal kitchens. That population of internal refugees included 200 children of school age. One of the children, fourteen-year-old Memory Phiri, explained that she had been unable to attend school since her house was submerged by the floods, a month earlier.

This misery could have been avoided had the local authority built the needed drainage infrastructure way back in 1978 or even a little later. The residents of Kanyama continue to suffer from preventable diseases brought on by unsanitary conditions. These diseases of course multiply during the hot rainy season when floods are likely to occur.

The most important resource in building a drainage system is labour. In addition, piping, stone, sand, cement, and excavation equipment are also required. All these are available in Zambia. Why then has the Kanyama drainage system not been built, as required by Zambian town and country planning law? Given the regularity of the flooding and its consequent predictability, why are the authorities always taken by surprise when floods occur? There has been no lack of opportunity for both levels of government to end Kanyama's vulnerability to flooding.

This vulnerability is well known. What is less publicised is the fact that a Zambian controlled firm of architects and property developers in South Africa did offer to convert Kanyama into a properly serviced residential area with proper drainage. When the offer was initially made, the Zambian government, while appreciating the benefits of such a project, expressed concerned that the Opposition, which controlled local government, might be given too much credit for the improvement in the standard of living for Kanyama residents.

Subsequently, President Mwanawasa was convinced that rebuilding shanty towns as outlined by the South African firm would be a good thing for the country. He therefore directed the firm to send the plans to him for action. The plans were sent but the President claimed not to have received them. The head of state then suggested that perhaps the project documentation should be handed to the Zambian mission in Pretoria and marked for the attention of the first lady. Mr Mwanawasa was convinced that this way the documentation would reach him. He was right. The documents were sent promptly to State House and Differ Mulimba, the president's special assistant, confirmed receipt of the plans.

Confirmation of receipt of the documents was the only good news the property developers heard from the state. No further action was taken by the government.

The Kanyama experience represents sins of both omission and commission on the part of Lusaka City Council. Alas this is not the only local authority to be seemingly indifferent to the health and welfare of citizens.

A Canadian mining company with a large operation in the north-western town of Solwezi has been attempting to build a clinic in the town for the past three years. The clinic is meant primarily to serve the mining community and would be seen as an integral part of the mining infrastructure for the management of work-related injuries and illnesses. It would allow employees and their dependents access to a very high level of primary health care. Among other services, the clinic would give HIV/AIDS care to both the mining population and the broader community as a registered facility through which government supported Anti Retroviral Therapy could be obtained.

The facility would in fact be more than a clinic because it is designed to have an eleven bed capacity, in addition to possessing emergency, x-ray, pharmacy, dental, maternity/birthing, and small procedures departments. Furthermore there would be a mortuary, laboratory, two consultancy rooms, a treatment room, and a private wing consisting of an overnight stay room with en suite and doctor's consultation room.

The mining company's vision goes beyond provision of medical services, however, as the intention is to develop a working relationship with local health facilities to build capacity for the management of health emergencies.

One would expect both the Solwezi Municipal Council and the Zambian government to jump at the opportunity of spreading high quality health care, especially given the fact that the construction of the clinic would involve no expenditure on their part. Sadly, that was not the case. While senior officials in the ministry of health showed some enthusiasm for the project, the general machinery of government proved an effective stumbling block.

The mining company needed title to the land where the clinic was to be built. The local authority indicated that the necessary approvals could only be granted by the central government. The central government in turn advised that it needed a recommendation from the local authority before issuing a certificate of title. It was also suggested that the certificate of title could not be issued until a new town plan for Solwezi was in place. The supportive officials at the ministry of health were in the meantime baffled as to why the two levels of government could not talk to each other and resolve this seemingly uncomplicated matter for the benefit of the country. Eventually the ministry's efforts paid off and title to the land was given in 2009, allowing the mining company to start construction. Even so, the inordinate delay suggests a failure to understand the country's developmental priorities which include health, as well as a failure of initiative. Failures to prioritise and take the initiative are not uncommon in today's Zambia.

Laws must be obeyed

There is no shortage of examples of gross negligence and disregard of the law to the detriment of the Zambian population. Zambian officials, like other members of the general population, must understand that choosing which laws to obey is not an option. All laws and regulations must be obeyed.

Laws are essential to economic development. The bylaws, for example, that are being routinely disregarded are essential in the overall regime of property ownership. Title to land may be issued, corruptly, but will afford little or no protection to the holder if it is issued in violation of zoning laws. The title will not enhance economic development either, as prudent lenders will decline to use the title for collateral purposes. The holder of the title will thus be unable to raise capital and start a business.

Disregarding bylaws in effect removes legitimate regulation from socio-economic activity and invites anarchy. This is not to advocate excessive regulation but rather to call for enactment and equal enforcement of relevant and necessary regulation. It is necessary to have town planning regulations; it is necessary to regulate the sale and purchase of farming land so that farmers can have secure title and be able to borrow against that title; it is necessary to regulate occupation of residential properties so that people can be secure in their ownership of homes; it is necessary to regulate the conduct of people in residential areas so that citizens can be safe and live in dignity. The reasons for good and necessary regulations are almost endless. In general, good and relevant laws provide the framework for sustainable economic growth.

But it is also important that public officials whose salaries are paid by the taxpayer be prudent in the use of public money. They should further make it their duty and responsibility to constantly look out for opportunities for Zambia and exploit those opportunities in the interests of the country. Elected officials and other public servants can set the tone for the entire country. They have a privileged position in Zambian society and will necessarily be looked on as role models. If they behave responsibly, responsible behaviour will quickly become the norm in the country. The requirement is that decision-makers play by the rules as well as reward those who play by the rules. Being negligent and indifferent is costly to Zambia. The end result of irresponsible behaviour and persistent negligence is societal collapse.

CHAPTER 5

CHANGING THE NATIONAL CULTURE

It is clear from the preceding chapter that Zambia needs to undergo a significant change in culture in order to forge ahead and becomes a prosperous nation. Changing the culture of any nation is a challenge. The challenge is especially acute in the case of Zambia whose current culture emanates from forty years of mismanagement and neglect.

The Zambian culture matches the style and comfort zone of the first president of the republic, Kenneth Kaunda, who seemed to have difficulty relating the success of the private sector to the provision of social services. His pronouncements consistently suggested that a vibrant private sector stood in the way of social progress. He firmly believed that it was possible for the state to provide every citizen with free education, free health care, and subsidised food. All this could be done without a vibrant private sector. The traditional role of the private sector, in Mr. Kaunda's view, could be performed successfully by state enterprises.

The effect of Kaunda's vision was to seriously disrupt entrepreneurial development in the country, and to undermine Zambians' sense of personal responsibility. The not infrequently asked question of the time was: "Why should I bother if I am not allowed to work for myself and the state will provide my basic needs anyway?" The state companies that were meant to generate the profits that Kaunda counted on for the country's development generally failed, at least partly because many of the managers hired to run these companies had to demonstrate a commitment to Kaunda's vision in order to be employed.

In 1964 Kaunda's government inherited a relatively sophisticated and strong economy. Indeed the immediate post independence years saw impressive economic growth in Zambia. The relative prosperity of the time however masked many policy deficiencies and allowed the injurious culture to grow.

Even informed Zambians were comfortable with the Kaunda culture. Only recently has it dawned on Zambians that culture might be, at least in part, responsible for the country's underperformance. The slowness in connecting culture to socio-economic performance is not uniquely Zambian. Most countries that have undergone change have done so only after the occurrence of a significant event. In the case of Zambia it is the unmanageable debt and widespread poverty that have encouraged a re-examination of the post-independence culture.

But simply recognising that Zambia's culture is partly or even largely responsible for the country's poor performance is not enough; steps must be taken to change the offending culture. And the time to do so is now because of the increasing recognition that the country's culture needs transformation. Change is certainly possible although it will require political commitment matching that demonstrated by the first MMD government in 1991 when the free market was once again legitimised.

Cultural change can be brought about both behaviourally and constitutionally. How political leaders interact with one another, for example, can raise the quality of political discourse and encourage civility in the general population. On the other hand adopting the right constitution can increase transparency, reduce mismanagement, and encourage personal responsibility.

The vituperative exchanges that have characterised the relationship between President Rupiah Banda and the leader of the Opposition Mr Michael Sata have done nothing to elevate the level of debate or increase civility. On the contrary the sight of the two leaders hurling abuse at each other (on one occasion each claiming to be less ugly than the other) has been dispiriting to the reasonable and encouraging to the uncouth who have found themselves in distinguished company, for once. Abusive exchanges between the leaders, typically unsupported by evidence, have done nothing to encourage thoughtful and responsibly communicated political intercourse.

It is no accident that both President Banda and Mr Sata cut their political teeth during the Kaunda era.

Civility and self esteem

Zambians are probably the most placid people in the world. But their country is today home to the nastiest form of politics. Why is there such a chasm between the people's behaviour and the behaviour of politicians? The answer lies in culture. Most people in Zambia are still guided in their daily lives by traditional Zambian culture which emphasises civility. Politicians on the other hand are guided by a political culture developed largely during an era of intolerance.

The one party era did not only disallow formal opposition to the government, it also dealt severely with opposition to the leader from within the Party. Verbal abuse against 'dissidents' was often used as a way of discouraging the general population from taking seriously utterances of people seen as disloyal to the Party. Those who lived during the era will recall how liberally lavatorial verbs were used to discredit real or imagined opponents of the regime. It was not uncommon for the UNIP hierarchy to quickly call for the 'flushing out" of dissidents. This would usually follow the declaration of the political offender, by the head of state, as either a 'stupid idiot' or 'malcontent'.

In effect the one party regime permitted the bullying of political opponents, and even allies who seemed to take a different viewpoint on a particular matter. Although the language of politicians moderated slightly after the return to democracy, Zambia does under President Rupiah Banda appear to be going back to the era of verbal abuse and intolerance.

Political incivility is on the rise again perhaps because the leadership often chooses to ignore bad behaviour and sometimes even indulge in it. In 2008 President Banda summarily dismissed two junior ministers while addressing a crowd of cadres from his party. The crowd was delighted by the news and some of them openly and jubilantly called for the fired duo to be physically assaulted. The president did nothing to restrain this behaviour. He certainly did not condemn it.

During the August 2009 by election at Chitambo, verbal abuse degenerated into a fist fight between a deputy minister in the office of the vice president and a member of one of the opposition parties. Again there was no reprimand from the government leadership. There was however a welcome expression of concern from a ruling party member of parliament. Ng'andu Peter Magande, former finance minister in the Mwanawasa government, informed the national assembly that recent incidents of violence in the country were worrying. Mr Magande was also critical of attacks on journalists by his own party's cadres. In Magande's view, Zambia had entered a period of "rising intolerance to one another".

Mr Magande, who had challenged Rupiah Banda for the MMD presidency a year earlier, is not as influential in the ruling party as he once was. In keeping with the culture of exclusion, he was not listened to by his own party when he issued the statement on political violence.

Less than a fortnight after Mr Magande's warning, a young member of the Patriotic Front opposition party was savagely attacked at the Lusaka High Court building. The victim's blood-drenched face was captured vividly on the front page of the independent newspaper, The Post. One reader of the paper later lamented, "Surely, the UNIP days are back, where those with different opinions are regarded as enemies".

Almost a year later President Banda appeared to confirm the reader's fears when he cautioned voters in the Western Province constituency of Luena that they would not get any development under his government if they re-elected the leader of the opposition Alliance for Democracy and Development Charles Milupi to parliament, just as UNIP used to do. Banda's warning was issued on July 27, 2010.

The previous year, during the run up to a by-election in Kasama, President Banda joined the fray in a most unseemly manner. His entry into the campaign was ominous from the beginning when the Patriotic Front mayor of the town stated publicly that the head of state could look forward to a hostile reception in Kasama. This statement of course went against established etiquette which requires local authority leaders to be courteous and civil to the head of state and other dignitaries visiting their jurisdictions. But whatever sympathy the mayor's unfortunate remarks generated for the President, quickly dissipated when Mr Banda likened the overweight candidate for the Opposition to a "bag of mealie meal". Mealie meal is the name given to corn flour from which the country's staple food is made. The President's speech consisted almost entirely of negative remarks and verbal abuse directed at the opposition candidate. The pattern continued when a few days later, the President digressed from his speech to refer to opposition members of parliament who were driving by as "lunatics".

In fact President Banda has taken the country back to the era of intolerance and disrespect of the most basic tenets of governance. The president certainly has difficulty understanding the concept of a non-partisan civil service. President Banda's failure to respect the role of the civil service has had disastrous consequences on the ground.

On February 16, 2010 the Post newspaper reported that the Northern Province permanent secretary, Mwalimu Simfukwe, had ordered civil servants in the province to vote for President Banda in the election scheduled for 2011. The reason given by the province's most senior public servant for this directive was that Banda was "their source of bread and butter."

In Mr Simfukwe's view public service workers were obliged to vote for President Banda because "they owed their jobs to President Banda's government."

This kind of language of course breeds an atmosphere of intolerance and even violence. It is perhaps not surprising that earlier, in mid January 2010 the President had again failed to condemn violence when his Works and Supply Minister Michael Mulongoti supported calls by young members of the ruling party to physically assault George Mpombo a former MMD defence minister opposed to what he considered unconstitutional tendencies in the ruling party. The youth wing of the party was threatening to physically prevent Mr Mpombo from attending the party convention.

In a remarkable show of intolerance Mulongoti declared that "a nuisance should not be allowed to attend the convention but only those who were in right standing with the party.

The words of the MMD cadres were even more unsettling:

> This is 2010; Mpombo should not even attend the convention because we will cut off his legs and all those who are insulting President Banda will not be spared.... We will beat them one by one like lizards coming from a hole.

There was however a voice of reason from within the ruling establishment. The MMD national secretary reminded his party that violence as a way of settling political disputes was unacceptable in a democracy. Too bad these words did not come from the president.

If the majority of Zambians are still guided by traditional values emphasising civility, why do they not bring pressure to bear on the politicians and demand more polite political dialogue? The answer lies in the fact that too many Zambians have a poor self image which often leads to the belief that their views cannot possibly matter. The poor self image and lack of confidence stems from both the colonial experience and the failure of post independence Zambian leadership. Whereas the colonial government dedicated itself to proving the inferiority of black Zambians in comparison to white British people, the inability of independent Zambian governments to deliver has been used as 'proof' that black Zambians are indeed inept.

This view is held not only by those white Zambians who opposed independence in the first place, and now take pleasure in the failures of the young state, but remarkably even by some black Zambians. The unholy alliance between these white champions of ethnic particularism and unsophisticated Zambians serves to reinforce the idea of uniquely Zambian ineptness.

Zambia has certainly not been as well governed as it could have been. It is also true however that Zambia was not the first country to be mismanaged. European history is replete with examples of mismanagement.

Indeed the European standard that most of Zambia's critics point to as the ideal in governance is a relatively recent phenomenon. For example, the modern state of Portugal goes back to at least the 12th century, with almost all its current borders being established in 1249. And yet Portugal did not become a democracy until after the Carnation Revolution of 1974, more than seven hundred years after the founding of the state. Experience with democracy before that had been a dismal failure, with the First Republic lasting only 16 years, from 1910 to 1926. This was an era that saw a dangerous undermining of parliamentary institutions largely as a result of widespread corruption and economic mismanagement. Portuguese reaction to the military coup d'être that ended the First Republic in 1926, was not unlike Zambian reaction to the Luchembe coup attempt of 1990.

Zambia has underperformed for a number of reasons such as the colonial legacy and inept post colonial governments. The country has not underperformed because Zambians are uniquely incapable of governing themselves.

But allegations of unique ineptness on the part of Zambians have had the effect of manufacturing a group difference which has played a huge part in demoralising Zambians and denting their collective self esteem. Because of repeated claims that Zambians are inept, many Zambians have actually adjusted their behaviour to comply with this stereotype. The psychological effects of this kind of conditioning are real. I shall rely on my friend Steven K. Baum to explain these effects. In *The Psychology of Genocide* Baum recalls the well known Jane Elliott experiment and explains how people can be conditioned into feelings of superiority and inferiority. The following is from pages 40 to 42 of his book:

> Jane Elliott discovered the powder [keg] of social identity among school children. The setting was 1968, the day after Martin Luther King had been shot. In the White, Protestant enclave of Riceville, Iowa, Elliott's demonstration was soon to become a classic experiment on manufactured groups and prejudice.
>
> Elliott knew that none of her students had met a Black person. She subsequently queried the kids about what they knew about Black people. Their responses: "They're dirty." "They don't smell good." "They riot." "They steal." "You can't trust them." "My dad says they'd better try not to move in next door to us."
>
> Next she divided the class into two groups - those with brown eyes and those with blue eyes. Anyone outside these categories, such as those with green or hazel eyes, was an outsider, not actively participating in the exercise. Elliott told her children that brown-eyed people were superior to blue-eyed, due to the amount of a colour causing chemical, melanin, in their blood. Elliott said that blue-eyed people were stupid and lazy and not to be trusted. To ensure that the eye colour difference could be made quickly, she distributed strips of cloth to be fastened around the neck.
>
> The "brown eyes" gleefully affixed the cloth-made shackles on their blue eyed counterparts. She withdrew the classroom rights of blue-eyed students, such as drinking from the water fountain or taking a second helping at lunch. Brown-eyed kids received preferential treatment. They bossed around the blues and were given an extended recess. Elliott recalls, "It was just horrifying how quickly they became what I told them they were." Within thirty minutes a blue-eyed girl had regressed from a "brilliant, self confident carefree, excited little girl to a frightened, timid, uncertain little almost-person."
>
> The brown-eyed children excelled under their newfound superiority. Elliott had seven students with dyslexia in her class and four of them had brown eyes. On the day the browns were "on top" those four brown-eyed boys with dyslexia read words that Elliott "knew they couldn't read" and spelled words that she "knew they couldn't spell." Prior to that day her students hadn't expressed any thoughts about each other based on eye colour.
>
> Elliott soon saw her brown-eyed students act like "arrogant, ugly, domineering, overbearing White Americans" with no instructions to do so.

> She understood that racism is learned - carefully or not. She then reversed it. "I made a mistake" she informed the class. "It was the blue-eyed children who are better!" Within minutes the blue-eyed children began acting like their brown-eyed superiors and the brown-eyed children assumed depressed attitudes. Elliott had taught them it was okay to judge one another based on eye colour, but she did not teach them how to oppress. "They already knew how to be racist because everyone of them knew, without my telling them, how to treat those who were on the bottom," says Elliott.
>
> For years when Elliot repeated the experiment, parents would call the school principal with invariably the same complaints: "I don't want my kid in that nigger-lover's classroom!"

In 2004 World Bank economists Karla Hoff and Priyanka Pandey reported the results of an Elliot-like experiment they had done in India. It involved 642 11-to-12-year-old boys from disparate villages in India. Half of the boys were high caste and the other half were low caste. All the boys were given the task of solving mazes. In the first exercise the boys did the puzzles unaware of each other's caste. On this occasion the low caste boys slightly outperformed high caste boys, solving almost six mazes compared to the high caste boys' five-and-a-half.

When the experiment was repeated, each boy was asked to identify his caste publicly. On this occasion, the high caste boys solved just over six mazes while the low caste boys solved just over four. The lesson drawn from the exercise is that performance and behaviour can be deeply affected by the way a group feels it is perceived and judged by others.

Zambians, like all dark skinned people, have been treated and judged harshly on the basis of colour for a long time.

Thus toward the end of the colonial era, the British government spent five times more on the education of white children than it did on the education of black children. That was the closest the colonial government came to closing the gap in education spending between 'European' children and 'African' children. As P.D. Snelson has pointed out in *Educational Development in Northern Rhodesia, 1883-1945*, the total amount spent on educating black children between 1924 and 1945 was £875,000 Sterling, the bulk of which came from the poll tax paid by indigenous Northern Rhodesians.

In comparative terms, the government spent £40 per white child in 1945 and £1.30 per black child. It is not surprising therefore that at independence in 1964 Zambia possessed fewer than 100 black graduates and 1,200 black School Certificate holders. Snelson describes this as "an inexcusably tiny store of educated manpower on which to draw for the development of a new state."

We shouldn't be surprised then that the new state floundered. We should however be concerned that Zambia's failures were attributed to the 'African stereotype'.

The negative racial stereotypes referred to by Elliott's children could have come from White Northern Rhodesians and even from White Zambians. Certainly the British settlers would have shared this view of the world almost from the inception of colonialism.

A great deal of absurd and foolish statements have been uttered and believed about dark skinned people for a very long time. In the book *Which Way Africa?* Basil Davidson quotes an Italian traveller who reported from the oasis of Tuat in 1447 that, "The peoples beyond the Sahara breed greatly, for a woman bears up to five at a birth." In my lifetime I have heard it claimed that Africans do not have the same emotional attachment to family as do Europeans. I have also heard it said that Africans mourn the loss of family members more deeply than Europeans. In both instances there is an attempt to manufacture difference and reinforce prejudice. Claims that Africans have limited feelings are usually made to justify harsh treatment of the people of the continent.

This was the case during King Leopold's rule over the Congo. It also was the case during the slave trade when devaluation of African life reached unprecedented levels. In response to the inhumane treatment that African slaves were being subjected to, some humanitarian groups in Europe began to complain to both the British government and the traders themselves about this inhumanity. The British government while sympathetic at some level nevertheless declined to intervene immediately on the ground that the trade was too profitable for Britain. The actual statement to this effect was made in 1775 by Lord Dartmouth, the Secretary of State for the Colonies. The even more callous response of some Liverpool slave merchants seventeen years later has been well documented by Davidson. It is as follows:

> Africans being the most lascivious of human beings, may it not be imagined that the cries they let forth, at being torn from their wives,

> proceed from the dread that they will never have the opportunity of indulging their passions in the country to which they are embarking?

According to the Liverpool merchants therefore, the screams on the slave ships had nothing to do with the fact that previously free people were now in captivity and had been taken away from their families; instead the screams were a result of fear by the captives that they may never again have sex!

More recently, high HIV infection rates in many African countries (including Zambia) have led to the quick judgement that Africans are indeed exceptionally promiscuous. The fact that the virus is spreading the fastest in Eastern Europe is either under-reported or explained away as a result of drug abuse, never sexual promiscuity. More surprising in an era of great information on genetic science is that very little has been said about the connection between genetics and AIDS. Some international development agencies have however drawn a strong link between AIDS and poverty.

There is in fact no basis upon which to conclude that Zambians are unusually promiscuous and therefore more immoral than other nationalities.

In this regard there is a revealing study done by the London School of Hygiene and Tropical Medicine that is noteworthy. Zambians would do well to pay attention to this study before they swallow uncritically what foreigners say about them.

The ground breaking study, providing the first comprehensive analysis of sexual behaviour around the world, was published on October 30, 2006 in *the Lancet*. The paper analysed data from 59 countries worldwide in an effort to answer questions about sexual behaviour, such as when people are introduced to sex, how many sexual partners they have and whether they practise safer sex. The findings of the study surprised many in the Western world. In general, the study concluded that, contrary to frequently expressed fears, there has in fact been no universal trend toward earlier sexual intercourse and promiscuity.

Perhaps of more interest to Zambians is the finding that it is the developed nations that reported comparatively high rates of multiple sexual partnerships, not countries like Zambia which tend to have higher rates of HIV infection.

This finding led the authors to suggest that social realities such as poverty, mobility and gender (in) equality may be stronger factors in sexual ill-health than promiscuity.

While monogamy was found to be the dominant pattern in most regions of the world, in African countries men were more likely to have multiple partners than women. But in some industrialised countries the proportions of men and women reporting multiple partnerships were more or less equal, suggesting that women in industrialised countries may be more promiscuous than their African counterparts.

Trends toward earlier sexual experience were found to be less pronounced and less common than is sometimes supposed. In the majority of countries, the age at which women were starting to have sex had increased. In African and south Asian countries, the trend toward later onset of sexual activity among women has coincided with the trend toward later marriage.

It has to be noted however that in Kenya and Zambia the sexual health benefits of marriage for women are offset by a higher frequency of sex, lower rates of condom use and their husbands' risky behaviours. Of course many husbands in the industrialised world engage in extramarital sex, as the study has shown, but this behaviour rarely translates into HIV infection because rates of condom use are generally higher in industrialised than in non-industrialised countries.

Genetics also provide an answer to the prevalence of AIDS in countries like Zambia. Scientists now understand that a gene which apparently evolved to protect people from malaria increases vulnerability to HIV infection by 40%. People of African descent have a variation of the "DARC" gene which may interfere with their ability to fight HIV in its early stages. The Cell Host and Microbe study by British and American scientists says the gene accounts for millions of extra HIV cases in sub-Saharan Africa.

The London School of Hygiene and Tropical Medicine study involved a huge amount of work and intellectual investment in the pursuit of understanding a human problem. This kind of effort is not always possible.

And yet it is precisely this kind of effort that Zambia must make to educate her population, change the culture of neglect and raise the country's collective self esteem.

Even with evidence from this study however, the world at large continues to explain the HIV/AIDS problem in Zambia and other

African countries in much the same way as Elliott's children would have explained away the misfortunes of the 'inferior' eyes.

But the children in the Jane Elliott experiment were subjected to prejudice for only a few hours before adopting feelings of inferiority. Zambians and other dark skinned people have been subjected to the most vicious forms of racial prejudice for centuries.

People treated in such an appalling fashion are bound to suffer from phenomenal low self esteem. Even more dangerous perhaps is the fact that over the years the negative stereotype attached to their kind becomes internalised, so that the victims of harsh prejudice themselves begin to behave in a manner consistent with that stereotype.

This appears to have happened in Zambia. Although a minority of sophisticated and well educated Zambians appear to have liberated themselves from feelings of ethnic inferiority, too many nationals are still burdened by the phenomenon. These feelings have translated into a belief that non-Zambians are necessarily more valuable than Zambians.

In mid July 1990, a British nurse working in Iraq was freed from a 15-year prison sentence for helping a journalist who was suspected of espionage and subsequently hanged. Daphne Parish was 53 at the time and her release was a result of pleas by President Kaunda to Saddam Hussein the then leader of Iraq. Immediately upon her release Ms Parish was flown in a private jet to Lusaka where she was met by Zambian officials and Iraqi diplomats. She was then driven to State House, the President's official residence, where she spent the night. Meanwhile back in Iraq, the Deputy Foreign Minister Nizar Hamdoun confirmed that Ms Parish's release was "in response to an overture from President Kaunda and for purely humanitarian reasons."

Mr Kaunda was the hero of the moment, earning rare praise and expressions of gratitude from Margaret Thatcher, the British Prime Minister. Certainly Kaunda had invested a huge amount of time securing the release of the British nurse. It is unfortunate however that he was not equally interested in a problem closer to home.

At the time President Kaunda was appealing for Daphne Parish's release, Webster Kayi Lumbwe a former officer in the Security and Intelligence Services and Ministry of Foreign Affairs was serving a twenty-year prison sentence for espionage. Lumbwe was tried secretly on the charge that he had passed on classified information to America's Central Intelligence Agency (CIA). The twenty-year sentence was the minimum sentence for the offence. When Lumbwe's appeal in 1986 failed, his family and friends intensified their efforts to persuade President Kaunda to release the cerebral former intelligence officer on humanitarian grounds. For a long time these appeals fell on deaf ears. Subsequently however Kaunda did pardon Lumbwe and other political prisoners in the wake of the Luchembe coup attempt, and also in response to a pointed question by the Christian newspaper, *the National Mirror,* which drew parallels between the Lumbwe and Parish cases.

The release of Lumbwe was well received but in the context of the Daphne Parish episode, it raised uncomfortable questions about the value the head of state placed on the lives of his own citizens. Kaunda had invested a huge amount of time and political capital to secure the release of a white prisoner in a far away land, but had chosen to ignore pleas for the release of one of his own countrymen whose circumstances were not too different from the Briton he staked his political reputation on.

A conscious effort must be made to educate Zambians about their worth. Like Ms Elliott's 'superior' children Zambians need to be told that they are valuable and as good as anyone else.

On the domestic political front, politicians must understand that the people are the masters and these masters need to be treated with respect. Too many Zambian politicians treat the citizenry as just an inconvenience that stands between them and lucrative political office. Being respectful of citizens also means promoting courteous political dialogue.

President Banda in particular can use his office to end political violence by condemning all acts of political misbehaviour and rewarding courtesy. As his predecessors have done before him, the current president holds regular press conferences at State House. These conferences have long been a way of communicating with the nation. They also represent an opportunity to change the country's political culture. The president has the power to create new rules of political discourse and conduct that could reinforce the value of open and respectful debate.

In his daily activities the president can also use the information he comes upon to applaud good political behaviour. He can do so by repeating positive news highlighting good behaviour, and ignoring malicious gossip.

The benefits of good political behaviour are not limited to politicians. The general population is inevitably affected by the conduct of political leaders. Good behaviour on the part of politicians acts as an incentive for ordinary citizens to be courteous and respectful in their own discussions with fellow nationals. When politicians are careful and respectful in their dialogue with allies and opponents alike, the public take political intercourse seriously and understand that they are respected and valued. In these circumstances the proposition that every opinion is valuable becomes self evident. Indeed it goes without saying that every person is valuable and should be valued. That is precisely the environment that makes it possible for self esteem to flourish.

Respect for the Zambian Individual

But self esteem can only benefit the nation if it translates into a collective desire by nationals to be responsible masters of their destiny. There is a requirement for the state to signal its trust and confidence in its citizens. That is not what has happened in the past.

Zambia needs to enter an era of personal responsibility. In this era the individual will be entitled to unqualified respect from the state. In return the individual will take full responsibility for his or her actions. It will be understood that rights entail duties and privileges entail responsibilities.

This approach would change Zambian culture significantly and increase the likelihood of the country prospering. Thus our driver from Mpima would know that it was his responsibility not only to start the journey to Lusaka on time but also to ensure that the vehicle was in good working order. Our Roma fire crew would be prepared at all times to respond to emergencies and ensure that they had all necessary equipment and resources, including water, to extinguish fires. ZESCO officers would know that it was their responsibility to secure all power lines and cables to ensure that they caused no harm. Police officers would understand that it was their duty to treat suspects with respect, while prosecutors would take it as a given that all were equal under the law and that prosecutions could not be done on a selective basis.

Local authorities would ensure that town and country planning laws and related regulations were routinely enforced for the benefit for the entire community.

The new culture would also mean the state broadcaster which cannot afford proper janitorial services but is proud to buy a luxury four wheel drive vehicle for its chief executive officer, has the sense to reassess its priorities and perhaps spend $20,000 less on the chief executive's car and invest the saving in janitorial services.

The Constitutional and social Framework

The change in culture will not however be sustainable without a constitution that supports and reinforces the idea of personal and collective responsibility. That responsibility must be palpable at all levels of government. Certainly people elected to parliament must be placed under an obligation to behave responsibly and to act primarily in the best interests of their constituents. That is not the case at the moment, given the dominance of the executive branch in the legislature.

In addition to constitutional change the social and economic structure of the country needs to change so as to focus on economic security and prosperity for nationals. The educational system too must be redesigned so as to prepare students for productive life in a competitive global economy. A combination of constitutional and educational reform should result in greater social cohesion, which is necessary for prosperity.

The following chapters will develop these themes further.

CHAPTER 6

GOVERNING WITH EQUITY

Zambia has never been governed on the basis of a constitution created by the people of the country for the benefit of all citizens. Typically constitutions have been drafted and amended under the guidance of the executive branch with a view to serving the interests of identifiable sections of the community rather than the country as a whole.

The pre-independence constitution, under which the 1962 general election was fought, was designed to minimise the likelihood of the nationalist parties seizing power outright. That constitution thus gave disproportionate electoral power to the white settler community.

The 1964 constitution had broader participation in its formulation than its predecessor, but even this document was not truly a creation of the Zambian people as it was negotiated by the British government, the nationalist leadership, and representatives of the white settler community. The public at large was not meaningfully engaged. The constitution did nevertheless protect basic human rights and define structures and powers of government.

It has already been pointed out that the 1972 constitution served the purpose of preserving the power of the United National Independence Party (UNIP) and its leader Kenneth Kaunda. There was no opportunity for the Zambian public to oppose the establishment of a one party state and this fact undermined the legitimacy of the nationwide consultation exercise the preceded the creation of the second republic.

The 1991 constitution was a product of the Constitution Commission of Inquiry which was appointed in 1990 under the leadership of Professor Patrick Mvunga. The 1991 document reintroduced political pluralism and ushered in the third republic. Although the ratification of the constitution was preceded by an inquiry, the urgent political circumstances of the day were such that no comprehensive and all-encompassing discussion could take place. UNIP's rule had become untenable but there was no lawful manner of retiring the autocratic government. A new dispensation was needed immediately. Despite the tight timeframe within which a new basic law of governance had to be produced, the Mvunga constitution reversed some of the losses made during the one-party era. Indeed this is the constitution that made it possible for the then opposition Movement for Multiparty Democracy to legally contest the 1991 presidential and parliamentary elections.

Although Professor Mvunga is better known as an academic lawyer, at the time he chaired the Commission of Inquiry, he was serving as Zambia's solicitor general and was thus a member of the executive branch of government. It is typical for the executive branch to seek to control the constitution making process, and the branch usually does this by ensuring that one of its representatives heads the commission of inquiry. This pattern was relaxed however after MMD came to power and appears to have been abandoned altogether by the Mwanawasa government.

Before coming into power, the MMD had undertaken to change the hastily drafted 1991 Constitution and to replace it with a new dispensation that would be broader based and non-partisan. Thus on 22 December 1993, the new Zambian president asked the respected lawyer John Mupanga Mwanakatwe to head what came to be known as the Mwanakatwe Constitutional Review Commission. Mwanakatwe had previously served as Minister of Education and Minister of Finance in the first and second republics. At the time of his appointment however he was not a member of the government.

The Mwanakatwe Commission had broadly defined terms of reference which included recommending a system that would ensure that Zambia was governed in a manner that would promote the democratic principles of regular and fair elections, transparency and accountability, and that would guard against the re-emergence of a dictatorial form of government.

The Commission undertook an extensive tour of the country soliciting views from the citizenry. The citizens did not disappoint and expressed their views without restraint as befitting a people who had recently been emancipated. There was overwhelming support for the view that a presidential candidate must receive 50 per cent plus one of the votes cast, for him or her to be declared a winner. The population also seemed to favour adoption of the new constitution by way of a constituent assembly attended by representatives of all political parties, civic society, trade unions, women's groups, churches and many others, on the basis that this would ensure maximum consensus. In addition the desire that the final document should be approved in a referendum was expressed.

By the time the Mwanakatwe Commission reported, the MMD had been in power for almost five years. The new president and his team were now less keen on transparency than they had been just a few years earlier. The White Paper following the Commission's report rejected the idea of a constituent assembly and a referendum. It also rejected the 50 per cent plus one recommendation with respect to presidential elections. Furthermore, the government declined to consider the introduction of new personal rights and the creation of a constitutional court and a more independent electoral commission.

By abandoning its 1991 promise to introduce a constitution that would strengthen individual rights and freedoms, and lessen the powers of the executive, the Chiluba government missed an opportunity to remedy Zambia's historic constitutional ills. In contrast, the government was quick to accept the regressive recommendation that a presidential candidate had to be born from parents who were citizens of Zambia by birth. Far from being 'non partisan', this provision was aimed at preventing Kenneth Kaunda, who had recently come out of retirement, from contesting the 1996 general election.

Despite expressions of serious concern about the new constitution, Chiluba's government proceeded to give effect to its White Paper by amending every part of the 1991 Constitution save for part III, which governs protection of fundamental rights and freedoms of the individual, and requires a national referendum to be amended.

The stage was thus set for yet another constitutional review commission. Zambians still needed a durable constitution that would allow them to be governed with equity.

Less than 18 months after President Chiluba's term of office came to an end, the new Zambian leader, Levy Mwanawasa, announced the appointment of yet another constitutional review commission. He called upon civil society groups to nominate members to sit on this commission.

The new commission was led by a British-trained lawyer who had previously served as president of the African Development Bank. Although Willa Mung'omba sat in the Zambian parliament in the 1970s, he has never been a member of the executive branch of government. In her essay on Discrimination and the Law pertaining to Immigration, Susan Margaret Clayton has suggested that "Mung'omba is the first chair of a constitutional review process that has not been in the executive or under executive direction, which may lend a measure of independence and therefore credibility to his commission." Incidentally Clayton notes that Mung'omba was designated chairperson, not chairman. She is delighted by the gender awareness on the part of President Mwanawasa!

Like the Mwanakatwe inquiry, the Mung'omba Commission toured the country extensively, and obtained a wide range of views from people. Its interim report and draft constitution were presented in 2005.

It is noteworthy that the Commission recommended adoption of the draft constitution by a constituent assembly and thereafter approval by the general population in a referendum. Like the Mwanakatwe Commission and in keeping with the wishes of most of civil society, the Mung'omba exercise also recommended that a successful presidential candidate should obtain 50 per cent plus one of the votes cast, in order to be elected. In the event of none of the candidates obtaining this, a re-run should be held between the two frontrunners.

Deliberations on the Mung'omba draft constitution have continued, but the government's response thus far has been that the Constitution of Zambia clearly states that the legislative power of the Republic of Zambia is vested solely in Parliament, and that it does not provide for the adoption of the constitution by a constituent assembly.

With respect to the 50 per cent plus one recommendation, the government has justified non-adoption of the clause on the ground that electoral reruns are costly and add to uncertainty.

Even so, the government did establish the National Constitutional Conference to discuss the Mung'omba Commission recommendations. The NCC proved to be an expensive venture at least in part because of the lavish allowances given to members and witnesses. In light of this it is difficult to argue that a constituent assembly is unaffordable. Nevertheless the Mwanawasa approach has been more promising than his predecessors'.

The Current Constitution

Even as we hoped that the NCC would finally produce a durable constitution, the reality is that Zambia is still governed by the flawed 1996 constitution.

The Constitution of the Republic of Zambia is the supreme law of the land. It is the foundation and source of the legal authority underlying the existence of the Republic. For this reason the constitution should consist more of declaratory principles than prescriptive provisions. It should go no further than providing the framework for the organization of the country and the relationship of the government to the citizens, and to all people within Zambia. The constitution ceases to be a framework when it becomes too prescriptive and reads like ordinary law. Too much prescription makes a constitution overly rigid and incapable of 'living' and soon leads to dissatisfaction and demands for new constitutional dispensations. An overly prescriptive constitution, especially one crafted with a view to addressing the interests of specific individuals rather than society as a whole, cannot stand the test of time.

On the other hand, a constitution that confines itself to principles that ensure liberty and maximum freedom for citizens, and that provides an objective and non-intrusive framework for the organisation of the country as well as the relationship between the governors and the governed, will typically receive universal acclamation.

This perhaps explains why the American Constitution has lasted for so long. The original United States Constitution adopted on September 17, 1787, by the Constitutional Convention in Philadelphia, and ratified by conventions in each US state in the name of "The People", had only seven articles. In more than 230 years of the American republic, the US Constitution has been amended only 27 times. The Constitution remains the shortest and oldest written supreme law still in use by any nation in the world today.

In contrast Zambia's constitution has 139 articles organised in thirteen parts. It is not my intention to analyse each and every one of these articles. I shall simply highlight some of the many worrisome provisions in Zambia's fundamental law.

Citizenship Provisions

Reflecting the interests of the white settler community that liked the idea of continuing to live in Zambia but that also wanted the protection of British citizenship should the new country fail or be hostile to their community, the 1964 Constitution bestowed citizenship on every person who was a British protected person by virtue of having been born in the former protectorate of Northern Rhodesia before independence. The Constitution also confirmed the citizenship of people born in Zambia after independence. The fact that no feminists were involved in negotiating the 1964 Constitution is evident from the fact that people born outside Zambia of a Zambian mother and a non-Zambian father were not entitled to Zambian citizenship.

In 1972 the Zambian political elite was no longer able to contain the opposition and was preparing to turn the country into a one party state. With this came a mistrust of the European secularist ideas incorporated into the 1964 Constitution.

The advocates of the one party state were increasingly anti-European and xenophobic in their views. It is not surprising that in 1972 Mainza Chona, the head of the National Commission on the Establishment of a One Party Participatory Democracy in Zambia, reported that most petitioners "felt that Zambian citizenship should be acquired through descent only and that citizenship by registration or naturalisation should be discontinued". In defiance of the established principle that birth guarantees citizenship, the Chona Commission also recommended that children of foreigners born in Zambia should only be able to acquire citizenship by way of formal application when they attained the age of majority. The reason for this recommendation was to prevent people born in Zambia but with no connection to or interest in Zambia from becoming citizens.

The 1973 Constitution did remove the sexist provision with respect to those born outside Zambia to a non-Zambian father. Now people born outside Zambia could claim their Zambian citizenship if at least one of the parents was a Zambian citizen. This victory for equality was however quickly undermined by another provision that restricted recognition of citizenship for children born in Zambia to alien parents to circumstances where the children's fathers were permanent residents. Thus a child born in Zambia to a resident mother and non-resident father could not become a citizen of the republic.

The 1973 Constitution is an example of the folly of limited consultation and too much reliance on the executive branch of government in crafting the country's supreme law. It is also an example of an overly prescriptive constitution. The following are the citizenship provisions in the Zambian Constitution:

4. Citizens of Zambia

(1) Every person who immediately before the commencement of this Constitution was a citizen of Zambia shall continue to be a citizen of Zambia after the commencement of this Constitution.
(2) A person who was entitled to citizenship of Zambia before the commencement of this constitution subject to the performance of any conditions following the happening of a future event, shall become a citizen upon the performance of such conditions.

5. Children of citizens of Zambia

A person born in or outside Zambia after the commencement of this Constitution shall become a citizen of Zambia at the date of his birth if on that date at least one of his parents is a citizen of Zambia.

6. Persons entitled to apply to be registered as Citizens

(1) Any person who --
(a) has attained the age of twenty-one years; or
(b) has been ordinarily resident in Zambia for a continuous period of not less than ten years immediately preceding that person's application for registration; shall be entitled to apply to the Citizenship Board, in such manner as may be prescribed by or under an Act of Parliament, to be registered as a citizen of Zambia.
(2) An application for registration as a citizen under this Article shall not be made by or on behalf of any person who, under any law in force in Zambia, is adjudged or otherwise declared to be of unsound mind.

(3) Parliament may provide that any period during which a person has the right to reside in Zambia by virtue of a permit issued under the authority of any law relating to immigration shall not be taken into account in computing the period of ten years referred to in paragraph (b) of clause (1).

7. Powers of Parliament

Parliament may make provision for --

(a) The acquisition of citizenship of Zambia by persons who are not eligible to become citizens of Zambia under this Part;

(b) Depriving any person of his citizenship of Zambia:

Provided that a person shall not be deprived of their citizenship except on the grounds that --

(i) That person is a citizen of a country other than Zambia; or

(ii) That person obtained such citizen by fraud.

8. Citizenship Board

Parliament may make provision for the establishment of a Citizenship Board to deal with any of the matters falling under the provisions of Articles 7.

9. Cesser of citizenship

(1) A person shall cease to be a citizen of Zambia if that person

(a) Acquires the citizenship of a country other than Zambia by a voluntary act, other than marriage; or

(b) Does any act indicating that person's intention to adopt or make use of any other citizenship.

(2) A person who --

(a) Becomes a citizen of Zambia by registration; and

(b) Immediately after becoming a citizen of Zambia, is also a citizen of some other country; shall, subject to clause (4), cease to be a citizen of Zambia at the expiration of three months after such person becomes a citizen of Zambia unless such person has renounced the citizenship of that other country, taken the oath of allegiance and made and registered such declaration of their intention concerning residence as may be prescribed by or under an Act of Parliament.

(3) For the purpose of this Article, where, under the law of a country other than Zambia, a person cannot renounce his citizenship of that other country that person need not make such renunciation but may instead be required to make such declaration concerning that citizenship as may be prescribed by or under an Act of Parliament.

(4) Provision may be made by or under an Act of Parliament for extending the period within which any person may make a renunciation of citizenship, take oath or make or register a declaration for the purpose of this Article, and if such provision is made that person shall cease to be a citizen of Zambia only if at the expiration of the extended period that person has not then made the renunciation, taken the oath or made or registered the declaration, as the case may be.

10. Interpretation

(1) For the purpose of this Part, a person born aboard a registered ship or aircraft, or aboard an unregistered ship or aircraft of the Government of any country, shall be deemed to have been born in the place in which the ship or aircraft was registered or in that country, as the case may be.

(2) Any reference in this Part to the national status of the parent of a person at the time of the birth of that person shall, in relation to a person born after the death of his parent, be construed as a reference to the national status of the parent at the time of the parent's death.

(3) For the avoidance of doubt, it is hereby declared that a person born in Zambia before the 1st of April, 1986, whose father was an established resident shall continue to enjoy the rights and privileges, under, and shall remain subject to, the law prevailing immediately before that date.

In contrast, this is how the United States Constitution declares citizenship rights:

> All persons born or naturalized in the United States, and subject to the jurisdiction thereof, are citizens of the United States and of the State wherein they reside. No State shall make or enforce any law which shall abridge the privileges or immunities of citizens of the United States; nor shall any State deprive any person of life, liberty, or property, without due process of law; nor deny to any person within its jurisdiction the equal protection of the laws.

The Zambian Constitution continues to permit citizenship by registration although the prescribed period of prior residence has been varied from four years in 1964 to ten years. The longer period of residence is a result of concerns expressed by petitioners who made representations to the Chona Commission. As has been pointed out, the extent to which these petitioners could be said to be representative of the country is doubtful. Even so, their xenophobia has continued to be reflected in the constitution and has also found its way into the Draft Mung'omba Constitution which extends the residency period to twelve years. In the Draft Mung'omba Constitution a foreigner wishing to become a Zambian citizen can either be 'lawfully resident' or 'ordinarily resident' in Zambia for the prescribed period.

The registration provisions in both the current constitution and the Mung'omba Draft Constitution ignore the realities of the global economy, apart from being unfair to both the country and the prospective citizen.

Successful countries understand that the challenge of attracting the best human capital is much greater in the global economy than it has been in the past. With increased mobility of labour the competition between countries to attract the best and the brightest has become fierce. By making it difficult for skilled foreigners to become Zambian citizens, the Zambians are in effect telling the world that any country can fish in their waters but they won't fish in other countries' waters. In other words Zambia is deliberately limiting its ability to recruit the talent necessary to propel it into the technological era while at the same time being indifferent to losing the talent it already has, to foreign countries.

Many foreigners enter Zambia with a view to doing skilled work or investing in businesses. The foreigners who like Zambia and contemplate taking out citizenship, have to wait for ten years before they can legally do so. During that ten year wait, they can of course change their minds and perhaps leave the country, taking their skills with them. They certainly will avoid making long term investments, and they will externalise as much of the income they earn in Zambia as possible.

On the other hand, if foreigners were allowed to apply for citizenship after four years residence, as was the case under the 1964 Constitution, it is likely that virtually all of them would buy homes in the fifth year of residence, in addition to making other investments. Thus the country would see a reduced rate of foreign remittances as naturalised Zambians find it necessary to spend more money at home.

The current policy of discouraging foreigners from becoming Zambian citizens as soon as possible continues to be costly to the country. Since independence Zambia has remitted abroad hundreds of millions of dollars on behalf of expatriate labour. That money could have been invested at home, for the benefit of all Zambians.

In contrast, Canadians have no doubt that they benefit from immigration and consequently the vast majority of people landing in the country do so as permanent residents. It only takes three years of continuous residence for a permanent resident to be eligible for Canadian citizenship.

There is no shortage of evidence to show that new Canadians invest quickly and significantly in their new country. Those who favour long periods of residence before foreigners can naturalise and become citizens argue that future Zambians must demonstrate their loyalty to the country and demonstrate to the authorities that they will not bring injurious cultures to Zambia. Zambia should certainly do all it can to avoid the importation of such social ills as apartheid, racism, and religious fanaticism. The assessment of suitability of would-be citizens can however be effectively accomplished by citizenship examinations. Canada not only has a points system that qualifies candidates for residency but it also has an examination for residents who wish to take out Canadian citizenship. The United Kingdom has also recently introduced an examination for prospective new Britons. This is one way of ensuring that new citizens understand the values of the society they are joining.

In any case foreigners in Zambia are routinely screened by the Ministry of Home Affairs for suitability as residents. It should not be too difficult to assess which of these foreigners have the potential to be good, law abiding and productive Zambian citizens.

One more point about the registration provisions of the constitution. Even after the residency period has been satisfied, the foreigner seeking Zambian citizenship cannot be considered for registration until he or she attains the age of twenty-one. The age requirement appears justifiable only in the historic context and has little bearing on today's reality. The age of majority in Zambia is eighteen. Why then should a person deemed mature enough to vote not be able to apply for citizenship?

Dual Nationality

The One Party Constitution specifically prohibited dual nationality and thereby further alienated Zambia from the international community. The more enlightened Mung'omba Constitutional Review Commission has however recommended that dual nationality should be allowed for Zambian citizens born to a Zambian parent who is a citizen by birth. Thus Zambians by registration or naturalisation may not, under the Mung'omba proposals, be allowed dual nationality.

While the Mung'omba approach represents an improvement on all previous constitutions save the 1964 one, it does raise concerns of its own. The Mung'omba recommendation effectively creates two classes of citizens, contrary to the spirit and letter of the 1996 constitution which guarantees equality of treatment for all citizens. Zambians by birth are accorded a superior status to Zambians by registration. As Clayton has pointed out, it makes no difference whether the Zambians by registration reside in Zambia or whether Zambians by birth reside abroad at the time they acquire dual nationality. Clayton fears that if implemented this provision could "breed resentment, discourage real integration and entrench anti-immigrant sentiments." These are not hollow fears. Most civil wars are started as a result of perceptions that one group is favoured over another. This was indeed the cause of the anti colonial independence movement in Zambia.

It is time for Zambia to grasp the nettle and allow dual citizenship for all nationals regardless of ancestry. In addition to facilitating freer movement of Zambian skilled labour and better dissemination of information, dual nationality would have other more tangible economic benefits.

Opponents of dual nationality cite security considerations and what they see as an absence of economic benefit to the country as reasons for not permitting non-indigenous Zambians from acquiring Zambian citizenship in addition to the citizenship of their countries of birth, as well as disallowing indigenous Zambians from acquiring additional new citizenships. With respect to security considerations, the basic argument is that it is impossible to determine the loyalty of people with multiple citizenships. At its most alarming level this argument goes on to suggest that dual nationality increases the likelihood of espionage.

There is in fact no evidence for this proposition. The best known case of betrayal and disloyalty in the British Commonwealth is that of three Cambridge graduates who served in the British foreign office.

In 1951 two British diplomats, Guy Burgess and Donald MacLean, disappeared and surfaced in Moscow five years later. The speculation was that the head of the Soviet section of the British Secret Intelligence Service had alerted Burgess and MacLean before they could be arrested for espionage. Indeed Harold "Kim" Philby had alerted Burgess and MacLean, as speculated. The three Cambridge graduates were the most successful spies recruited by the Soviet Union.

Burgess and Maclean as members of the British Foreign Office supplied secrets, including highly classified nuclear information as well as secrets relating to the formation of the North Atlantic Treaty Organisation (NATO). Philby joined MI-6 and eventually served as head of counterespionage operations after World War II and became the top British intelligence officer in Washington in 1949.

At the time of Burgess' and MacLean's disappearance in 1951, Allied counterintelligence had begun to suspect Maclean was a Soviet mole. Philby got wind of this and told his friend Burgess to pass on the information to MacLean. Both Burgess and Maclean immediately fled to Moscow. Philby had saved his friends, but his close association with them soon directed attention to himself. He was relieved of his intelligence duties in 1951 and dismissed altogether from MI-6 in 1956. By 1963 it was clear that counterintelligence was close to nabbing him, so he too fled to the Soviet Union.

Kim Philby died in Russia in 1988, and was buried with full honours in a Moscow cemetery.

Burgess, MacLean, and Philby were British nationals with a traditional British education. Not one of them held another citizenship apart from their birth nationality.

And yet they betrayed their country. They took their citizenship for granted, as indigenous people tend to.

In Zambia the best known espionage case is perhaps that of Webster Kayi Lumbwe. That case has already been referred to. Suffice it to say here that Lumbwe was an indigenous Zambian who held no other citizenship. The notion that there is an axiomatic relationship between dual nationality and propensity toward espionage is plainly absurd. It is equally absurd to suggest in today's global economy that no economic benefits flow from dual citizenship.

Zambians in the Diaspora may not be looked upon favourably by some of their compatriots who accuse them of having 'abandoned' their country. In fact the Zambian Diaspora makes a quantifiable contribution to the national economy.

In October 2007, the International Fund for Agricultural Development, an arm of the United Nations and the Inter-American Development Bank, released the first complete map of worldwide remittances. The map compiled the best available information drawn from data collected on migrant populations, percentage of migrants sending remittances, average amounts remitted annually, as well as the average frequency of transfers. The map gets its credibility from the fact that central banks and other official government sources, money transfer companies, international organizations and academic institutions were used for reference support.

According to the map, Zambians in the Diaspora sent $201 million home in 2006. That represents 1.8 per cent of the country's gross domestic product, and is more than the government got from mineral royalties. The Diaspora does this under very difficult conditions. Zambia is one of the more expensive countries to send money to because of high bank charges. People now rarely send bank drafts to relations and friends at home because a $100 draft attracts a fee of $20. That is exorbitant. The result is that Zambians use money transfer companies and when it is not possible to do so they hang on to their money until they can find someone going home who would then physically deliver the cash. At the very least the high fess at home slow down the rate of remittance and sometimes encourage Zambian expatriates to abandon the idea altogether. But despite these difficulties the Diaspora continues to support the home economy.

The $201 million indicated in the map is probably an underestimate of the cash sent to Zambia by the Diaspora. Whatever the case, it is clear that those outside the country could send far more if the constitution allowed for dual nationality. The reason for this is that many well paying jobs in the countries to which Zambians emigrate are reserved for nationals. Permitting dual citizenship would enable Zambians to become citizens of the countries they emigrate to and therefore allow them to access these jobs. The increased income earned by the Diaspora would lead to increased remittances to Zambia.

There does appear to be a strong correlation between dual nationality and levels of remittances, as the Ghanaian and Indian experiences show.

In response to rising remittances from the Indian Diaspora at the turn of the century, the Indian government set out to effectively nullify the anti dual nationality provisions in the law.

On December 22, 2003 the Indian Parliament passed a bill that effectively allowed dual citizenship to people of Indian origin. The bill which became law from 2nd December 2005 has helped grant dual citizenship to Persons of Indian Origin (PIOs) belonging to, or having citizenship of other countries subject to certain conditions. The grant of dual citizenship was intended to facilitate easier travel to and from India for Diaspora members who had have taken foreign passports. It was also meant to encourage remittances from Indians abroad to their ancestral land.

The law appears to have worked. Whereas in 1996/1997 and 2003/2004 the Indian Reserve Bank reported remittances of $12.3 billion and $21 billion respectively, by 2008 these remittances had shot up to $45 billion.

We can be sure that with the introduction of this law Indians who had previously emigrated but held back from acquiring a second passport for fear of losing their Indian nationality, were now able to do so and thus open for themselves new opportunities that increased their ability to earn more and send larger remittances home. For Indians who had taken out new citizenships and thus lost Indian citizenship, the original nationality was effectively restored and the possibility of returning to the homeland became a reality. For these Indians it made sense to send money back home and build a nest egg for retirement.

The Ghanaian experience tells a similar story.

Ghana allowed dual nationality in 2001. In 1990 Ghanaians living abroad sent $200 million home. A year after the new law came into force, remittances jumped to $680 million. In 2003 the Ghanaian Diaspora demonstrated its appreciation of dual nationality by sending home a whopping $1 billion. Five years later that figure had doubled.

The Bank of Ghana figures are conservative because not all remittances go through official channels. The impact of the remittances, official or unofficial, is however beyond doubt. Ghana's building boom for example is attributed largely to these remittances.

Executive Branch

The role of the Executive branch of government is spelt out in 29 articles in Part Four of the Constitution. In contrast, only four sections in the US Constitution stipulate the role and responsibilities of the executive branch of government.

The concerns with the constitutional role of the executive branch of government however go beyond the overly prescriptive nature of the document. To start with there are serious restrictions on who may aspire to be president. These restrictions appear out of touch with the realities of today's increasingly global economy and geopolitics.

In addition to being a Zambian citizen, a person wishing to contest the Zambian presidency must be born to parents who are Zambians by birth or descent; must have attained the age of 35; must be a member of, or be sponsored by, a political party, must be qualified to be elected as a member of the National Assembly, and must have been domiciled in Zambia for at least 20 years.

It is both desirable and understandable that a Zambian president should be a citizen of the country. It is less understandable why that president's parents must either have been born in Zambia or been born outside Zambia to indigenous Zambians. Surely Zambians would be more interested in the abilities and commitment of their president rather than the origins of his or her parents. This requirement automatically excludes Zambians whose parents originated from say Malawi, the United Kingdom, or Zimbabwe.

This form of discrimination is surely unacceptable in a country whose constitution otherwise emphasises human equality and equal protection under the law. Furthermore the discriminatory treatment of

Zambians with Malawian, British or Zimbabwean origin completely ignores Zambia's geopolitical history. Zambia is a landlocked country surrounded by, among others, Malawi and Zimbabwe. Indeed between 1953 and 1963 Zambia, Zimbabwe, and Malawi constituted a federation. Even before the declaration of the federation, many Malawians and Zimbabweans chose to work and live in Zambia. Many married locally and raised children who had no other culture than the Zambian one. These children are as Zambian as can be.

Zambia is also a former British colony and inevitably had a significant population of British people introduced to it during the colonial era. By independence time a significant number of these people had in fact been born in Zambia.

While the general behaviour of British settlers may not have been admirable, this cannot be justification for xenophobic constitutional provisions which seek to exclude non-Black Zambians from citizenry. There is such a thing as birthright.

The arguments raised in favour of restricting the presidency to indigenous Zambians are usually identical to the arguments raised against dual nationality. These arguments have already been addressed. Suffice it to say here that the purpose of a constitution is to set the basic rules for election of presidents, not to actually elect those presidents. The Zambian constitution is so restrictive with respect to election of presidents that it actually undermines the very purpose of having elections. Election of leaders is the preserve of the population. We have hustings precisely for the purpose of assessing the suitability of candidates.

For the same reason, it may be time to revisit a provision borrowed from the US constitution which requires presidential candidates to reach the age of 35 before assuming office. This requirement stands in marked contrast to Zambia's life expectancy which stood at 39 in 2009. The more compelling argument perhaps for reducing the qualifying age is that there is nothing magical about the number 35. Many people have managed affairs of state at younger ages. For example, the person most familiar with the intricacies of modern government in Zambia at the time of independence was probably Valentine Musakanya. He was also arguably the most qualified person to lead the nation. And yet at that time, Musakanya was less than 35 years old.

There is little harm and much benefit from lowering the qualifying age from 35 to say 21. A reduced qualifying age will bring precocious talent into the political arena and increase political choice for the Zambian electorate.

Allowing independent presidential candidates to contest elections would also have the effect of increasing political choice and re-enfranchising those Zambians who feel that the platforms of existing political parties do not reflect their values.

Domicile

The Zambian constitution does little to increase choice with respect to presidential elections. In addition to citizenship, age, and other restrictions, a prospective presidential candidate is required to "have been domiciled in Zambia for a period of at least 20 years." The term 'domiciled' is not defined in the Constitution and it is noteworthy that the Mung'omba Draft Constitution avoids the use of the term altogether and opts instead for a requirement that the presidential candidate must be "ordinarily resident in Zambia for a continuous period of 10 years immediately preceding the election."

The usual legal meaning of the term 'domicile' is 'a place of permanent residence.' This definition however does not help clarify the residence requirements for a presidential candidate. The wording in the Constitution makes it possible for the governing party to disqualify a potential opposition candidate they deem to be a threat. For example, would a person born in Zambia of indigenous Zambian parents qualify for the office of president even though that person may have spent three of the last twenty years serving as a Zambian diplomat in a foreign country? Would the person be deemed to have been domiciled in Zambia despite the fact that he or she worked in say Brussels?

The advocates of this clause argue that it is necessary to ensure that a presidential candidate is familiar with the pressing issues of the day. Candidates cannot be familiar with these issues, the argument goes, if they have been absent from the country for a long time. The argument is fallacious. It would be absurd to suggest that Zambians who serve as their country's diplomats abroad are uninformed about events in Zambia simply because they have lived abroad for a few years. The absurdity of the argument is clear when one considers that a large part of diplomats' responsibilities is to educate foreigners about Zambia. In any case the point of election campaigns is at least in part to assess the level of understanding of issues by candidates. The campaign and not the constitution is the place to determine the suitability of candidates.

Even if the argument against Zambians who spend too many years abroad once had a grain of truth, it is surely time to abandon it now that the internet has made access to information so easy regardless of geographic location.

The only purpose this restriction now serves is to limit political competition faced by Zambia's ruling class. The provision in the Mung'omba draft constitution, although less punitive than the current clause, would do the same thing. It would exclude from participation in presidential elections a large number of highly qualified and sophisticated Zambians whose only crime was to seek further education and useful exposure in the broader global economy.

Let us imagine two young Zambians attending primary school in Chilubi Island. Both children do well in their examinations and enter a local secondary school. Shortly after completing school, one of the boys, whom we shall call Kaloba, decides to become a fisherman and is content to spend the rest of his life on the island. The other boy, whom we shall call Keenda, goes to university on the Copperbelt. After successfully completing his first degree Keenda decides to leave Zambia to do a Master of Sciences degree in London and subsequently a PhD at Edinburgh. Before completion of his studies, Keenda supports himself partly by writing for a British newspaper on southern African affairs. He also lectures undergraduate students on a subject called 'Indigenisation of Technology in Southern Africa'.

Under the current constitution Kaloba would be considered more qualified than Keenda to run the affairs of state in Zambia. Kaloba would thus be rewarded for never having ventured abroad for further education and work experience. In reality of course Keenda would be infinitely better qualified than Kaloba to be president of Zambia, and would stand a much better chance of placing Zambia on the road to sustainable prosperity than Kaloba ever could.

The Zambian constitution must encourage qualified men and women to serve their country at all levels of political life.

It must also discourage mediocrity which now results from unduly restrictive constitutional provisions. Such a constitution will not however emerge as long as politicians in power dominate the constitution making process. As already pointed out, each Zambian constitution has been crafted with a view to benefiting certain individuals at the expense of the rest.

Sadly the practice continues. Before President Mwanawasa's death, there was a move by MMD party activists to amend the Zambian constitution so that no person over the age of 70 could contest presidential elections. The target of that provision was Michael Sata, the populist leader of the Patriotic Front opposition party who narrowly lost the 2006 election, and even more narrowly the 2008 presidential by election, when he lost by 1 per cent of the vote. The by election took place after Mr Mwanawasa's death. His vice president, Rupiah Bwezani Banda, succeeded him. Mr Banda was already 70. It was no longer in the MMD's interest to amend the constitution as earlier demanded.

It did not take long however for the MMD to propose another amendment. This time the suggestion was that no one should stand for presidential office unless he or she had a university degree. Again the target was Michael Sata who, as far as was publicly known, did not have a degree.

Remarkably, in January 2010, the National Constitutional Conference adopted the clause requiring a presidential candidate to have a minimum of a bachelor's degree in order to contest an election. The Mung'omba Draft Constitution was also aware of the importance of ensuring a minimum level of academic accomplishment for presidential candidates but it proposed a grade 12 certificate or its equivalent, as the minimum requirement.

The proposed Article 123 clause 1 (e) stipulates that a person shall be qualified to be a candidate for election as President if that person has obtained, as a minimum academic qualification, a first university degree or its equivalent.

Commissioner Peter Machungwa spoke for the majority members of the commission when he said that it was important to have a republican president who was educated and able to function in today's technologically advanced world.

Thus our fictitious character Keenda would be deemed qualified to run for president while at the same time unqualified on account of the domicile provision. On the other hand Kaloba would appear to be disqualified from contesting the presidency. The matter may not however be that straight forward. The proposed Article 123 sets the minimum academic qualification as a university degree 'or its equivalent'. Supposing Kaloba went on to become a successful fisherman and set up a business that employed many people, not just in fishing but also in food processing. Supposing Kaloba also attended a number of seminars and workshops and actually wrote a book on entrepreneurship in a technologically advanced world. Would these experiences be equivalent to a university degree? There are many universities in North America that grant university degrees on the basis of what they call 'life experience'. Kaloba would appear to have enough life experience to satisfy the requirements for a degree from these universities.

Clearly the proponents of this clause did not think the matter through and rushed to adopt it in a clumsy attempt to prevent the leader of the opposition from contesting the presidency.

Mr Sata responded to the adoption of the clause by assuring the nation that this move would not thwart his political ambitions. Many in the country believe that in the face of evidence suggesting that the ruling party would go to absurd lengths to prevent him from running for presidential office, Mr Sata has been quietly studying for a degree over the past few years. Whether or not he has is no longer relevant as in late 2010, the National Constitutional Conference reversed itself and said it could after all accommodate presidential candidates who did not have university degrees.

An Independent Legislature and an Effective Executive

If the Zambian Constitution limits freedom of choice for the Zambian electorate, it also limits choice for the president when he is appointing members of his cabinet. As indicated earlier, the constitution requires members of cabinet to also be members of the legislature. Thus Zambia does not have a clear separation of powers between the legislative and executive branches of government. Experience shows that the integration of these two branches of government has not aided the aims of good governance and has in fact undermined democracy. All too often the government has dominated the legislative branch so much as to effectively make it a puppet of the executive branch. This has undermined the legislature's ability to debate freely and supervise government effectively.

The strong presence of the executive in the legislature encourages ruling party members of parliament, and even some opposition members, to seize every opportunity to support the government in the hope that such support will be seen as loyalty and lead to a ministerial appointment. Conversely, criticism of the government, however legitimate, is avoided. The effect of supporting the government unnecessarily and avoiding criticism of it has allowed all post independence governments to use the legislature as a rubber stamp, and harmed the national assembly.

But the executive branch is also harmed by the absence of a clear separation of powers. Save for the eight nominated members, parliamentarians are elected by constituencies. Although there is a certain amount of political sophistication and respect for ideology in urban constituencies of the Copperbelt Province, there is a serious lack of diverse political information and sophistication in rural and semi rural areas. In order to win in these constituencies, candidates must identify strongly with the area and be well versed in local issues. Often these issues are unique and quite different from national issues. A person elected in one of these constituencies and subsequently elevated to the cabinet will sometimes find it difficult to reconcile local interests with national interests.

This conflict often leads to the parliamentarian seeing him or herself as 'the people's champion' in cabinet. Many ethnic tensions, typically provoked by a development project being placed in one part of the country rather than another, have their roots in this perception. A clear separation of powers would avoid this problem by allowing the president to appoint to the cabinet any citizen, as long as that person was not a parliamentarian, member of the judiciary, civil servant, or otherwise legally barred from serving.

It should not be imagined however that parochialism only has deleterious effects in cabinet. The legislature itself struggles with many members who are unable to take a national perspective in their deliberations. But that perhaps is to be expected from a legislative body elected on the basis of geographical representation.

The first past the post constituency system works wonderfully in homogenous societies. It is less efficacious in young ethnically and culturally diverse societies like Zambia. And yet no constitutional review commission has ever looked at the way Zambians elect their parliamentarians. To be sure Zambians have more similarities than differences, but Zambia is also a young diverse country vulnerable to ethnic tension. The country's institutions must therefore promote national unity and minimise opportunity for ethnic tension. The way in which leaders are elected influences national cohesion.

One method of electing parliamentarians that may encourage national cohesion and discourage ethnic particularism in national political life, is the List System. Under this system, there would be no constituencies. Instead political parties contesting parliamentary elections would draw up lists of candidates to be presented to the entire nation. Thus electors would not vote for a single candidate but for a party.

Each party's list of candidates, ranked according to the party's preference, would be published on the ballot paper. After the voting each party would receive seats in the national assembly in the same proportion as the votes it won in the general election.

A threshold would have to be set by an independent electoral commission to determine the number of votes required to win a seat. In the case, for example, of a party fielding 150 candidates and winning 20 per cent of the vote, the top 30 candidates on the list would be assured a seat in parliament. A reasonable threshold for success would be around 5 per cent. The threshold encourages small parties to collaborate while keeping fringe parties out of contention.

The List system has worked well in South Africa, Israel, and most countries in continental Europe. The United Kingdom also used the List System for the 1999 European Election. In Zambia the system would have the effect of giving the same value to each vote in addition to guaranteeing a high degree of party proportionality. If a party receives say 40 per cent of the vote, then it would get 40 per cent of the seats in parliament. The system is also more user friendly for voters, whose primary responsibility would be confined to choosing one political party. It also helps smaller parties, with good messages but limited resources, to compete effectively as they are spared the need to visit every corner of the country, and instead rely on electronic and print media to tell their stories to the nation as a whole.

Furthermore, because the List would have been drawn up by political parties seeking to take power nationally, the system would encourage promotion of national rather than local (and possibly ethnic) issues. Similarly a government coming to power after such an election would be less inclined to 'punish' those constituencies that voted against it, as virtually every government in Zambia has done, because under the List system voters can vote anywhere in the country and thus make it more difficult to ascertain with certainty the voting patterns of particular communities.

For the List system to work best in Zambia however thought would have to be given to a review of the law under which parties are registered to ensure that they are inclusive and fully democratic.

The List system is worthy of consideration as Zambia prepares for a more genuine and transparent debate on its constitutional future.

It is hoped that that debate will take the suggestions made here into account. It certainly must consider, as the Mung'omba Commission did, the separation of powers between all three main branches of government. Furthermore politicians must be encouraged to understand that they are not the custodians of the long term. That is a role for the public service, a role which should be guarded jealously by an independent public service commission, responsible for merit based public service appointments aimed at attracting the most qualified talent available for positions in the civil service.

Governance with equity includes fairness to all. In its current form the Zambian constitution is far from fair to all.

CHAPTER 7

A Nation Not a Tribe

It is critical for Zambia that its constitution promotes cohesion and that its leaders behave in a manner that encourages nationhood and discourages sectarianism.

Zambia is a young nation consisting of a collection of historically independent kingdoms arbitrarily brought together as a result of European colonial enterprise. Some of these kingdoms like the Bemba and the Lozi had sufficiently centralised systems of government that in their day qualified them as nations. The people from each of these communities have a "common descent, history, language, etc., forming a State or inhabiting a territory." This definition is from the Oxford Dictionary of Current English. But these groups can no longer function as nations for a number of reasons, not least of which is their inability to control exclusive territory. These groups, like any other, must now be part of a modern Zambian republic that successfully incorporates the old indigenous nationalities. It is the Republic of Zambia that has sovereignty over all the territory known as Zambia.

The country's borders are only 100 years old and the modern Zambian State was only founded in 1964. Zambia is essentially a collection of indigenous kingdoms cobbled into one country as a result of the Berlin Conference of 1885 which allotted "spheres of influence" to the relevant powers and ushered in a period of unrestrained colonial adventure by the imperial powers of Europe, while simultaneously eliminating or at least diluting indigenous rule. The territory now known as Zambia was thus designated British.

Zambia cannot now revert to the pre-colonial era. Zambia must play as well as it can, the hand it has been dealt by history. The country must behave like a nation, not a tribe.

The fact that Zambia has entities within it that consist of people with strong bonds of identity such as a shared culture, history, language or ethnicity, need not take away from Zambia's legitimacy as the nation for all these entities. Zambia should not look at itself as a classical nation-state either because a nation state, in addition to having defined borders and territory, is a country of racially and culturally homogenous people. Thus in a classical nation state everyone would speak the same language, probably practice the same religion, with all these facets of national life being seen as a reflection of national values. Zambians speak many languages, although the claim that the country has 73 languages is an exaggeration. That number confuses language with dialect, and clan with ethnic entity. For example Bemba, Lala, Lamba, Swaka, Bisa, Ushi etc are essentially the same language. This language does however have dialectical variations. Similarly the speakers of these dialects are labelled as different "tribes" when in reality they belong to the same ethnic grouping.

While the promotion of these distinctions may be understandable in the colonial context, as a way of dividing the "natives", it is incomprehensible why today's politicians would continue to rely on this kind of inappropriate and divisive myth. Zambia does not have 73 languages. The country has seven linguistic groups, all of which belong to the Bantu family of languages. To draw differences between say Sala and Ila is rather like separating Cockney, Lancastrian, and Geordie from English. Politicians would be better employed emphasising that which binds Zambians than manufacturing differences.

Despite speaking many languages and dialects, the people of Zambia have a collective common history going back 100 years. That history has in turn provided opportunities for a common Zambian culture to emerge. Until the attainment of independence this new culture was most evident on the Copperbelt Province which acted as a melting pot for Zambians from all parts of the country and abroad. The Copperbelt agreed on a common language, Bemba, and adapted it to suit local conditions. Thus emerged what is sometimes referred to as Town Bemba, a language not unlike Lamba, the indigenous tongue of the land. The ease with which the diverse citizens of the Copperbelt Province intermarried helped consolidate their new culture.

For a while it did appear that this experience was going to be extrapolated to the rest of the country. Sadly the process was greatly slowed by the short-sightedness of politicians and their willingness to exploit ethnic differences for their own political ends.

Condemning exploitation of ethnic differences is not to deny the diverse nature of Zambia. Rather it is to acknowledge that while the nation may be diverse and relatively young it does nevertheless have a legitimate claim to statehood and nationhood. Being a legitimate state compels Zambia to behave appropriately as a responsible entity under both international and domestic law. For example, Zambia must do whatever it can to reduce statelessness, as required by international law. That imposes a duty on Zambia to have clear and non-discriminatory citizenship laws. The republic must also be dynamic and have a capacity to accept beneficial influences from abroad. This is perhaps the major difference between a tribe and a nation.

A tribe, defined by the Oxford dictionary as a group of primitive families or communities linked by social, religious or blood ties and usually having a common culture and dialect and a recognised leader, is usually exclusive and either unable or unwilling to seamlessly incorporate foreigners even for the greater good. A modern nation on the other hand accepts immigrants, is aware of the outside world, and does its best to compete in the global economy.

In multiethnic countries like Zambia, the interests of the 'tribe' and the interests of the nation do not always enjoy confluence. Indeed more often than not the two entities have conflicting interests. In addition to nations being more favourably exposed to outside influences, nations will also be less reliant on a chief with absolute executive power but will instead have a cadre of leaders functioning in different but inter-related spheres. The nation will furthermore have great leadership mobility. It has to be said too that a modern nation will appreciate diversity and understand that diversity leads to high performance, as it fortifies the free market of ideas.

So, Zambia's ethnic groups should not be seen as 'tribes', not only because of the absence of egregious primitivism warranting the use of the term, but also because so labelling these entities legitimises the inevitable conflict between 'tribe' and nation. Given Zambia's peaceful nature, it may be tempting to assume the inevitability of the nation and a corresponding belief that it will last forever. Successful nationhood is not inevitable. How long a nation lasts depends on how well organised and governed it is. For example, an undemocratic nation without a leadership succession process may collapse quite suddenly. This is essentially what happened to Yugoslavia, a nation that once had ties with Zambia and cooperated in a number of areas including nation building.

To be a more successful nation, Zambia must find a non-ethnic glue to bind its diverse population together. The task need not be unduly onerous given the Copperbelt experience. But the Copperbelt experience was driven by citizens, not the State. So, it is not so much the citizens who need to change their behaviour; it is the State. In this regard much needs to be done.

For short term political gain, politicians and other State actors have exploited ethnic differences for their own purposes. The trend was most noticeable during the One Party era when in the absence of ideologically competitive politics, many politicians turned to the ethnic group for legitimacy. Whereas in the pre-One Party years a politician who came from say the Eastern Province would be able to successfully contest election in the Central Province as long as he or she belonged to the more popular party, during the One Party era that candidate would be forced to contest only in the east as an individual within the only legal political party. In the circumstances, most candidates outside the Copperbelt Province and Lusaka retreated into their ethnic enclave and campaigned largely on the basis of ethnicity or cultural affinity.

Sadly the practice all too often rears its ugly head even after the country's return to democracy. During the presidential by election of 2008, the ruling party candidate Rupiah Banda travelled to his home province and publicly stated that he expected that region to vote for him as he was 'one of them'.

He further advised that other presidential candidates should look to their 'home provinces' for election. This was a remarkable statement for a person running for the office of President of the Republic of Zambia. It was also an example of how, against their own instincts, Zambians have been unduly sensitized to ethnicity, at the expense of nation building.

Official sensitisation

When he first came to office, Frederick Chiluba assembled one of the most multiracial cabinets in the world. He raised hope that Zambia was moving beyond ethnicity and making serious effort to quickly turn it into a nation that respected and encouraged diversity. In fact President Chiluba was as trapped in the politics of prejudice as most Zambian politicians. Addressing one of the early rallies in 1990 by his Movement for Multi Party Democracy, Chiluba declared that Zambia had "seventy-three tribes and if you don't belong to any of these then you are not a Zambian".

The immediate audience for this statement was Kenneth Kaunda whose parents had migrated from Malawi. Kaunda himself was of course born in Zambia and entitled to claim both Zambian nationality and Bemba ethnicity. There were people within the MMD who shared Kaunda's background but they were not singled out for attack because they happened to agree politically with Mr Chiluba. This is sadly a common feature of Zambian politics. Too often rules are applied selectively and used to denigrate opponents.

Equally worrisome is the fact that internal ethnic identity is used to confirm Zambian nationality. As Mr Chiluba suggested in his 1990 speech, one needs to belong to a 'tribe' in order to be Zambian. Thus a Zambian of British, Indian, or South African origin, born in Zambia of Zambian parents, cannot be a Zambian on account of not belonging to one of Zambia's indigenous ethnic groups.

This discrimination, in a country whose constitution purports to recognise the equality of all citizens, is not without consequences.

A childhood friend whom I shall call Sigo had a reputation for academic brilliance and patriotism. A year after Zambia's Independence he rejoiced when he learnt that the new country was going to build a university. I talked to him a lot about this as my father was the main fundraiser for the project in the Copperbelt Province, where we were both born. I left Zambia before the end of our high school days and was consequently not able to attend the University of Zambia which was now operational. But Sigo did attend and considered himself fortunate and privileged to be accepted by UNZA, as the University came to be popularly known. He was a proud, happy, and gregarious member of the university who participated in many extramural activities, particularly the kind that showcased Zambian culture. Coming from the Copperbelt my friend's first language was Bemba. But he also learnt Nyanja, the main language spoken in Lusaka Province, in addition to English.

As expected, Sigo easily graduated from UNZA and was sent abroad for post graduate training. While in England he was offered a permanent job but declined the offer on the basis that he preferred to work in his homeland. So he returned to Zambia.

I lost touch with Sigo and did not re-establish contact with him until many years had elapsed. When I saw him again he had lost much of his gregariousness and was quite subdued. His patriotism was also less evident. In fact I was shocked to learn that he now saved as much money as he could in foreign currency and avoided making long term investments in Zambia. What had happened?

About four years after his return from England Sigo had applied for a new passport. He was shocked when the initial application was denied and he was instead threatened with deportation. The deportation threat was never carried out but Sigo was obliged to appear before the Citizenship Board to formally apply for Zambian citizenship.

All this was prompted by the discovery by an immigration officer that Sigo's last name was Malawian. Since Sigo's last name was Malawian, he was deemed not to be an indigenous Zambian, and since he was not an indigenous Zambian, he had to apply formally for Zambian citizenship. Sigo described the entire experience to me as "most humiliating". He felt betrayed and unwanted in his own country.

While the feelings of humiliation have abated over the years, Sigo continues to feel unwanted and insecure. Each time he applies for a new passport, he is obliged like all applicants to complete an affidavit that among other things requires him to state his father's chief and village. He is also required to indicate his 'tribe'. Sigo has no 'tribe' or chief or village because he was born on the Copperbelt in an urban centre. His late father did have a connection to a chief and village but that chief and village are in Malawi. Far from being encouraged to celebrate his Zambian identity Sigo has been sensitised to internal ethnicity and pressured to think of his country not as one entity but as a dismembered society consisting of different ethnic entities.

With all the evidence we have, no society today should be encouraging ethnic identity, as Zambia is doing. There is no benefit in forcing Zambians to declare their ethnicities. On the contrary, the exercise is potentially dangerous, as the Rwandan experience demonstrates.

Unlike the situation in Zambia where colonialism resulted in a multi-ethnic society of many identities, in Rwanda the Hutu and Tutsi groups coexisted as essentially one people before the arrival of Europeans. The Hutu and Tutsi identities as we know them today are a creation of the Belgians. The loosely defined Hutu and Tutsi clans in existence at the advent of Belgian colonialism were turned into racial identities that constructed the Hutu as indigenous and the Tutsi as alien. The new racial classifications were enforced through state-issued identity cards, not unlike Zambia's national registration cards, that proclaimed the holder's race. Education and vocational training was determined by racial classification as indicated by the identity cards. On this basis the Hutu were excluded from the priesthood and local government.

But the Tutsi could become priests and participate in civic affairs. They were also favoured for promotion as commissioned officers in the army. Given this background, it is not surprising that the Hutu felt resentful and by 1959 waged a civil disobedience campaign that led to the pre-independence Social Revolution in which they overthrew the Tutsi monarchy and sent thousands of Tutsi fleeing into exile. Ironically the presence of so many Tutsis in exile reinforced the myth that Tutsis were alien to Rwanda. Thirty years later when the exiled Tutsi invaded Rwanda, the authorities whipped up 'patriotic' fervour by highlighting the threat of a 'foreign' Tutsi Diaspora population in Uganda, and set the stage for the common acceptance by the Hutu population that the Tutsi had to be eliminated as a race.

It is clear then that ethnic classification on identity cards in Rwanda instituted by the Belgian colonial government and sadly retained after independence was crucial in perpetuating ethnic identity. During the 1994 genocide a government-issued identity card with the designation "Tutsi" was all that was required for a summary death sentence to be carried out at any roadblock. Nothing aided the speed and magnitude of the 100 days of mass killing in Rwanda than the government identity card.

The Rwandan experience makes a compelling case for the avoidance of classification of ethnic, racial or religious groups on identity cards. Group classification on any official personal document subjects the holder of the document to profiling and human rights abuses based upon that person's group identity. In times of crisis such classifications make it easy to target individuals belonging to 'suspect' groups for abuse such as imprisonment and even death. Zambia needs to act now to eliminate these classifications from both the national registration card and passport application affidavit.

Language

The new national registration card in Zambia which obliges the holder to declare a chief and a village does nothing to bind the Zambian nation together.

Zambia must do nothing to threaten the fabric of the nation, and everything to strengthen that fabric. The country needs to adopt policies that will act as glue for the young nation.

Language could be one such glue. The recent debate on the adoption of Bemba as a national language revealed remarkable maturity by Zambians. The number of non Bemba speaking nationals who spoke in favour of the proposal was surprisingly high. Still, there were many Zambians who opposed the proposal. The opponents may not constitute a majority but they are a significant minority. For this reason their views need to be respected and given primacy. A simple majority would not be sufficient to make such a fundamental change as the declaration of the Bemba language as the national lingua franca of Zambia.

Opposition to the recognition of Bemba as a national language was largely a result of the fact that language in Zambia has been politicised. Gone are the days when the industrial conurbation of the country could settle on one indigenous language as their lingua franca. In 2011 Zambia is not able to emulate China which had no difficulty declaring Mandarin as the national language simply on the basis that that was the most widely spoken language in the country. The response of most Chinese people, who spoke Cantonese and other minority languages, was immediately to start language training in Mandarin.

For the foreseeable future however Zambia is unlikely to have an indigenous language as its main lingua franca. While the existence of such a language would be very helpful in forging a uniquely Zambian identity and strengthening nationalism, its absence need not end Zambia's hopes of unity. Zambia is not the only country in the world not to have an indigenous national language.

Even the United Kingdom which we think of as homogenous has at least four languages besides the dominant English. The Welsh language, for example, is enjoying something of a revival. There continue to be Gaelic speakers in both Scotland and Ireland. The Cornish language is not dead and may be heard in part of the southwest.

Despite the demise of the last 'native speaker' of Manx in 1974 the language is now strong in a revived movement of enthusiasts and has been taught formally in Isle of Man schools since 1992.

For an English speaker the existence of other languages in the United Kingdom may be moot given the dominance of English. But there are other countries whose linguistic diversity is as challenging as Zambia's.

In April 2010 King Albert II accepted the resignation of Belgian Prime Minister Yves Leterme's five-month-old government as a result of a language dispute. Belgium has three language communities, Flemish, French, and German.

The Leterne government was brought down as a result of a standoff between Dutch (Flemish) and French-speaking parties over language and political rights.

Belgium is a young country by west European standards, having been founded in 1830. We can only hope that by the time Zambia is 180 years old, it will have depoliticised language and found a way of moving forward and avoiding language-based strife.

A more successful example of multilingual coexistence is perhaps Switzerland which has four languages. German is the language spoken by the majority of the population while Rumantsch is spoken by only one per cent. The second most popular language is French followed by Italian. Switzerland has no serious language issues perhaps because of the highly devolved system of government which gives every Swiss a say in civic affairs regardless of linguistic and cultural affiliation.

Given Zambia's history, a useful model to study for effective language management may be *Jamhuri ya Muungano wa Tanzania* better known as the United Republic of Tanzania. Tanzania has 135 spoken languages but its official language is Kiswahili. English is also used commonly in administration and commerce. The Tanzanians are especially proud of the fact that they took a Bantu language, Kiswahili, and modernised it so that it could serve effectively as a national language. They boast, with justification, that theirs is the purest and most sophisticated form of Kiswahili.

Early on in his presidency, the country's founding leader, Julius Nyerere, translated William Shakespeare's *Julius Caesar* and *the Merchant of Venice* into Kiswahili, and now *Julius Kaisari* and *Mabepari wa Venisi* are Shakespearian staples in local schools.

Tanzanians' ability to communicate with each other in one common language owned by all of them has enhanced national unity greatly. The country is often praised for its unity and freedom from debilitating ethnic tension.

Can Zambia have its own Kiswahili?

Chizambia

The most challenging aspect of learning a new language is verb conjugation, as any student of French will attest. Verb conjugation is not however much of a challenge for a speaker of any Zambian language wishing to learn another local language. All Zambian languages have the same pattern of verb conjugation.

If a new Zambian language were to be created from the current crop of languages and dialects, the major issue would therefore be one of vocabulary rather than conjugation. Vocabulary is generally easier to learn than conjugation

The starting point in creating what I refer to as Chizambia would be the identification of common words in at least the seven main indigenous languages. The number of these common words is not insignificant. For example, the word for aeroplane, *Ndeke,* is the same in every spoken Zambian language. Another common word is *Kapokola* which means police officer.

Once the common words have been identified, the exercise would then concentrate on allotting meanings to existing words. It would be essential for the purpose of this endeavour to recognise language usage. By most accounts the most widely spoken indigenous language in Zambia is Bemba followed by Nyanja, Tonga, Lozi, Kaonde, Lunda, and Luvale.

The indigenous languages have not developed much since the advent of independence and it is probably accurate to state that the best Bemba, Nyanja, Tonga and Lozi literature was written, by Zambians, during the colonial era. Consequently, Zambia's indigenous languages do not adequately reflect the technological advances of the past half century. Even so, the Bemba and Nyanja languages have demonstrated a great capacity to indigenise new technological terms. While at Oxford, I was surprised to learn from an Englishman who had lived in Zambia that the Bemba language had a term for helicopter. According to Peter Esmond, the term is *chimunyungwi*. Peter went on to explain that the word also meant dragonfly. In this instance the architects of Chizambia would have to decide whether the term for helicopter would be borrowed from the Bemba. If they opted for

Chimunyungwi, then the Chizambia word for dragonfly would have to come from the Nyanja, which is the next most widely spoken language.

For Chizambia to be fully effective as a language, the linguistic architects would have to look at all indigenous languages and dialects as assets critical to the development of the new lingua franca. For example, in most local languages the word for doorway, entrance, gate, foyer, hallway, and reception, is the same. Under the proposed methodology of developing Chizambia, the word for doorway would come from Bemba, the word for entrance from Nyanja, the word for gate from Tonga, the word for foyer from Lozi, the word for hallway from Kaonde. Examples of other words that could be treated in like fashion are book, novel, treatise, thesis, novelette, logbook, diary, and novella. The difference with this group of words is that the architects of Chizambia would need to borrow from more tongues than the seven recognised indigenous languages; they would need to make use of dialects as well. The Chizambia words for diary and novella would have to come from two local languages not on the list of recognised indigenous tongues.

The idea of Chizambia is not to have a language that replaces and banishes the English language from use. English should continue being an official language of the country.

Chizambia's purpose would be to enhance national unity and preserve indigenous Zambian culture and identity through language. Zambia would thus become a bilingual country, linguistically comfortable at home and abroad.

Language not enough

It would take a very forward looking government to adopt Chizambia as the national language. Thus far no government has demonstrated that kind of vision. The hope must lie with the academic world which could perhaps develop the language and leave it on the shelf until the dawn of a more visionary and culturally aware era in Zambian politics.

Even if a national language for Zambia were to be adopted however, Zambia would still need to invest in other nation-building measures designed to create a collective consciousness and enhance national pride. In the pre independence era the Copperbelt province demonstrated that at least the indigenous Zambian groups could come together, adopt a common language and establish a common culture. There was both a collective consciousness and a national pride that turned the province into the most vocal advocate of Zambian independence.

The collective consciousness on the Copperbelt did not generally include the white settler community. Indeed this community overwhelmingly supported continued colonial rule and even local white rule. This, together with entrenched racism and the flaunting of unearned privilege convinced many black Zambians that whites could never be their compatriots. The few white people who supported Zambian nationhood were ostracised and often threatened with violence.

Andrew Sardanis has narrated this ostracism. Both Sardanis and Joe Shaw, a well known accountant and white Zambian nationalist received hostile receptions whenever they tried to persuade white settlers to support the independence movement. By and large the white settler community's privilege stemmed simply from skin colour; it was not earned.

Even the most uneducated, least entrepreneurial and quite pedestrian settlers employed domestic servants whom they referred to as 'house boys' and 'house girls', regardless of age. Their pre-school children often had a play mate called a *picannin*. This 'friend' would typically be a child of the 'house boy'. An important condition of service for the black child was never to argue with the child master.

The black child had to accept everything the white child master told him to do unless of course these instructions were overridden by the white child's parents.

This is the segment of the population that nationalists like Sardanis and Shaw had to persuade to support Zambian nationhood. It goes without saying that few were persuaded. On the contrary, conservative white settlers did a huge amount of psychological and physical damage to other white people supportive of the independence movement. The view within the nationalist movement that it should concentrate on the black vote and ignore whites altogether had no better fortifier than the collective white settler attitude toward the idea of democracy. White settler hatred for the independence movement had more catastrophic consequences however. In Livingstone, John Hunt, a supporter of the independence movement was so poorly treated when he attempted to make the case for independence before a conservative white audience that he was driven to depression and suicide. There is a street now in Livingstone named after him.

In the post-independence era white Zambians are often seen as agents of imperialism who had resisted emancipation and now look for every opportunity to denigrate the new nation and discourage it. They complain endlessly about the country, even as they continue to lead privileged lives they could never replicate in their 'homelands'. They are usually uninformed on the most basic issues about the country and are consequently taken by surprise when new pronouncements are made. Few whites in Zambia see themselves as nationals, rather they see themselves as Europeans living in Africa and are remarkably prone to the same nauseating generalisations about the continent we have learnt to expect from uninformed North Americans and Europeans. They tend to judge Zambia on the basis of this negative African stereotype manufactured by the western press, rather than on the Zambian reality.

White Zambians who grew up with the *picannin* mentality still find it difficult to interact with black people as equals. They still expect to have their way in the event of a conflict with a black compatriot. Equally black Zambians unfortunate enough to have the *picannin* disposition have great difficulty treating white people as equals and tend to give them the benefit of doubt in the event of a disagreement. For these black Zambians a normal relationship with their white compatriots continues to be elusive. They are either obsequious or very angry with them.

This background explains at least in part the widespread desire by many black Zambians for race-based exclusivity in matters pertaining to citizenship. As a modern nation however Zambia must take a broader and more legally sustainable view of citizenship. Excluding citizenship candidates on the basis of what some of their ancestors may have done, or even on the basis of the general stereotype of a group, is reminiscent of a tribal, not national, society. In any event if there is discrimination against certain groups for historical injustices, what are we to do about members of the same groups whose ancestors behaved appropriately or even suffered at the hands of their kin? Should Zambia not be open to John Hunt's descendants?

With respect to citizenship for the current crop of whites who live in Zambia, the fear is that allowing this group to acquire citizenship may entrench social ills like apartheid into the Zambian fabric. This argument has two main weaknesses. The first is that not all white people living in Zambia fit the negative stereotype of racism. Those who do not subscribe to this stereotype should surely have an opportunity to become nationals. The second weakness is that the argument assumes that the act of conferring citizenship is unsupported by process. Zambia can and should introduce a citizenship examination to ensure that future citizens share Zambia's best values and are knowledgeable about the country.

Strong people, Strong nation

Zambia is kept weak in part because of the unwillingness of its constituent parts to present a united front with a common resolve to prosper. The tension between black and white Zambians is an obvious example of disrespect, but there are other equally injurious relationships. For example, the wealthy - whatever their skin colour - tend to look down on the poor whom they see as hoards of irritants, rather than as potential assets. The employed looked down on the unemployed, the educated look down on the uneducated, and drivers look down on pedestrians whom they assume have absolutely no right to use public roads. All this contradicts traditional Zambian values which put emphasis on compassion and the protection of the weak. Today's Zambia is largely indifferent to the challenges and woes of the weakest members of society, and there is a clear and damaging tension between privileged Zambians and fellow nationals who happen to be underprivileged.

Zambian political leaders have of course claimed to be compassionate and even purported to adopt ideologies in proof of this compassion, but they have done so only for political gain. Thus Mr Kaunda's philosophy of humanism made some nice headlines at home and abroad, but the reality is that under the Kaunda regime, facilities for the elderly deteriorated, educational standards declined, prison welfare became almost non existent, and the number of political prisoners increased, as did the use of torture.

Kaunda's successor Frederick Chiluba did not fare any better. Vulnerable groups in society continued to be marginalised even as Mr Chiluba declared Zambia a Christian nation. He also presided over a machinery of corruption that resulted in hundreds of thousands of citizens doing without basic needs as the social service system failed to deliver, and in some instances collapsed altogether.

President Mwanawasa's 'New Deal' government committed itself to fighting corruption but corruption actually increased under the president's watch, all to the detriment of vulnerable Zambians.

President Rupiah Banda did not pretend to have an ideology but the deterioration in services for vulnerable groups continued. The treatment of prisoners is particularly shocking. Official indifference to the welfare of prisoners suggests that a convicted person loses basic human rights once a prison sentence begins. This attitude also affects people accused of committing crimes and awaiting trial in prison, even as the country's constitution declares that all are innocent until proven guilty.

The main prison in the Zambian capital is Lusaka Central Prison which was designed to hold 200 prisoners. Today, the institution has more than 1000 inmates with no corresponding increase in facilities. For most inmates, life at the prison is a living hell.

On April 30, 2010, the British Broadcasting Corporation reported on conditions at the prison focusing initially on an inmate who was serving a two-year sentence for selling marijuana. The inmate, given the name of Bright by the BBC, feared that he now faced a life sentence as a result of engaging in unprotected sex with the self-appointed captain of his prison cell. Bright was always hungry as the prison could only afford to feed him twice a day. So when the captain offered Bright extra food in exchange for sex, the former drug trafficker agreed, even though he had never had sex before with a man.

Despite the reality of male to male sex in prisons, the Zambian government continues to ignore appeals for the repeal of colonial era laws banning homosexuality. This has kept homosexual contact at a subterranean and therefore unregulated level, with detrimental consequences for society. An organisation called *In But Free* conducted a survey of prisoners in 1998 which suggested that 27 per cent of them were HIV-positive - eight points higher than the national rate at the time.

In light of this, Dr Oscar Simooya, the head of *In But Free,* has called for the legalisation of consensual male to male sex. He argues that society cannot successfully legislate against sex. Instead the government should recognise the reality of homosexual sex, be practical and take measures to prevent transmission of HIV.

He has asked that a policy of making condoms available to prisoners be considered, a position also supported by the medical director of the Zambia Prisons Service, Dr Chisela Chileshe. The policy cannot be considered however for as long as Zambian criminal law forbids homosexuality, so prisoners - guilty or innocent - continue to risk infection and if they do get infected, they spread the virus into the broader population when released from jail.

Merely changing the policy on condoms however is only one facet of a new policy regime necessary to enhance the status of prisoners and prepare them for a more productive life after on the outside. In addition to recognising the negative effects of unprotected sex in prison, the authorities must decongest Lusaka Central prison and other penitentiaries around the country. Prisoners too need space and even privacy to maintain their dignity. They should certainly pay for crimes they have committed but they should also be respected as human beings. People do not cease to be human beings just because they are incarcerated. The primary purpose of incarceration should be to reform erring members of society and to prepare them for a more productive life. Prisoners should one day look forward to making a positive contribution to society. In today's Zambia too many prisoners end up like Bright; they leave prison with a virus that threatens the health of society as a whole.

They also leave prison educationally worse off than when they went in because Zambian prisons offer no opportunity for educational advancement, in the absence of functioning libraries and teaching programmes. The Zambian government should look at prisoners as a captive audience ready for academic and vocational development; an audience that will leave prison in much better shape intellectually than they were in at the time of admission. This is what is expected of modern states.

Unlike a tribe, a modern state encourages its citizens to be strong and self reliant. The modern sovereign government therefore must meet certain basic conditions and responsibilities. A state fails when it does not meet these responsibilities.

The international organisation Fund for Peace is dedicated to promoting sustainable prosperity. In furtherance of its work, the organisation publishes an annual Failed States Index. The following is the criteria used by Fund for Peace to characterize a failed state:

- loss of physical control of its territory, or of the monopoly on the legitimate use of physical force therein,
- erosion of legitimate authority to make collective decisions,
- an inability to provide reasonable public services, and
- an inability to interact with other states as a full member of the international community.

  The criteria suggest that failure comes essentially from an inability to perform socially, politically, and economically.

Although Zambia's central government appears to have practical control over much of the country's territory, the state nevertheless comes perilously close to being a failure on account of the frequency with which democratic decision making is undermined, as well as the authorities' inability to provide public services. Another concern would be the government's ineffectiveness in combating corruption. The reader will recall that despite huge amounts of money being raised in 1978 to address the Kanyama flooding of that year, Kanyama settlement is still without a proper drainage system and therefore continues to be vulnerable to flooding.

The 2010 Failed States Index does not place Zambia in the 'Alert' category but it does place the country in the 'Warning' category, which is only one step away from the worst rating. Zambia cannot be successful unless and until there is an appreciation of the value of all citizens and a concerted effort to allow each citizen to realise his or her full potential. The country can only be as strong as its weakest citizen.

Impediments to viable nationhood

There are many reasons why Zambia struggles to turn itself into a viable modern nation. The treatment of indigenous ethnicity has already been alluded to. In addition to that, the absence of a politically neutral, professional, and secure public service, appointed on merit, has made nationhood that much more challenging.

It does not help either that so many of Zambia's critical decisions are made abroad by people who at best only have a theoretical appreciation of the country. The very image of Zambia is determined more by the foreign media than by local thinkers and writers. All Zambian governments have been content to have foreigners as final arbiters of how the nation is perceived by the world, while local journalists have been more concerned about reporting puerile mutual verbal abuse by incompetent politicians than by engaging in serious in-depth analysis of national issues. Even diplomats who are paid to represent Zambia abroad rarely respond to unfair negative articles appearing in the newspapers of countries where they are accredited.

For example, in 1991 as Zambia anxiously awaited the first democratic election after nearly 20 years of dictatorship, one Jonathan Manthorpe, a writer for Southam News confidently told his audience at home that Zambians were extremely worried about the forthcoming election and that foreigners were leaving the country in droves in anticipation of the inevitable violence. He then added that locals too would like to leave but were too poor to do so. Had Mr Manthorpe not relied on the aloof white Zambian ghetto for information he may have realised that ordinary people in landlocked Zambia have a long tradition of travelling to neighbouring countries, regardless of economic status. More importantly he may have realised that Zambians were in fact looking forward to the election and had no concerns about their safety in this regard. In the end Zambians showed up in record numbers to vote in an election declared by all concerned as free, fair, and peaceful! Zambians were not surprised by this. After all, they are only one of a handful of diverse young nations in the world never to experience civil war or military rule.

The Zambian mission in Canada, where Mr Manthorpe's damaging article appeared, offered no response to the piece.

Allowing foreigners so much say in the determination of the country's image is perhaps an inevitable consequence of Zambia's unhealthy dependency on international aid, which has increased the role of foreigners in practically all areas of governance and policy determination. It is also a consequence of the absence of a robust domestic economy capable of producing a prosperous middle class not dependent on government largesse and therefore sufficiently free not only to keep the government in check but also to counter anti-Zambian foreign propaganda.

The chapters that follow will assess the value of international aid as well as the desirability of a robust domestic economy.

CHAPTER 8

From International Aid to International Cooperation

Pride and a desire for sovereignty motivated the nationalist campaign for independence in Zambia. The nationalists, speaking on behalf of the majority black population, and even some minority interests, asserted with confidence that it was time for colonised Northern Rhodesia to transform into sovereign and independent Zambia with a seat at the international table.

Almost half a century after independence, Zambia is less sovereign, less independent and virtually with no international influence. Zambia is dependent for its economic well being on the international community, including the colonial power it considered unfit to govern its people in 1964. Zambia enjoyed more sovereignty and independence during the years 1964 to 1969 than it does today. The country also exerted an international influence at this time that was possibly disproportionate to the size of its population. Zambia was such an important country that in the late 1960s, the London Financial Times saw fit to have a correspondent covering Zambian affairs and based in Lusaka.

Lusaka was then abuzz with newly minted executives who confidently negotiated deals on behalf of their companies and country. The new university in Lusaka produced high quality graduates who had no difficulty continuing post graduate work at prestigious universities like Oxford and Harvard. The university itself was built partly with private Zambian funds raised from a broad spectrum of enthusiastic citizens.

Economic independence is now all but dead. In his 2010 budget, Finance Minister Situmbeko Musokotwane found it necessary as previous ministers of finance have done, to look to foreign donors for support. On this occasion 14.5 per cent of the national budget was raised from grants given by Zambia's so-called cooperating partners, while 13.1 per cent was financed through domestic borrowing. The percentage of the budget financed by foreigners may appear high but is in fact relatively low for Zambia, where international donors have traditionally financed between 20 and 30 per cent of the country's public expenditure.

The relatively low level of support in the 2010 budget appears to stem from donors' concerns about the Banda government's perceived reluctance to curb corruption, and not from deliberate government policy to reduce dependency on foreign powers.

Aid and Corruption

Receiving aid has become a way of life in Zambia. Utterances from political leaders suggest that begging no longer comes with a sense of shame. When more than $300m of health funding to Zambia's government was suspended by the Global Fund to fight Aids, Tuberculosis and Malaria, in June 2010, the reaction of the Zambian authorities was to condemn the Fund for endangering the lives of its nationals.

But it was not the Global Fund that had endangered the lives of Zambians, it was the Zambian government that had done so by tolerating corruption in the disbursement of grants by the health ministry. The Global Fund had in fact done everything it could reasonably be expected to do to avoid the suspension of aid. The director of communications for the Fund, John Liden explained to the BBC that the health ministry had failed to take the necessary corrective steps since corruption was first detected. In his words:

> We have identified a set of individuals; we have alerted Zambian government authorities about this. We have repeatedly asked for action, there has been slowness in action on the Zambian side. That's one of the reasons we feel we do not have confidence that the Ministry of Health, at this stage, can continue to channel funding of this magnitude for health in Zambia.

Sadly, this was not the first time that public money was misused or stolen. At about the same time as Global Fund assistance was being suspended, the European Union withdrew some funding to Zambia for road-building because of corruption. A year earlier, the Netherlands and Sweden halted $30m of direct aid for the Zambian health ministry because money was disappearing into the pockets of officials.

Another topic of conversation in Zambia in mid 2010 was the government's decision to take a Chinese loan to procure mobile hospitals. The decision was taken against the advice of civil society, including the health workers' union, and health experts. Despite these objections the government persisted in the venture and committed the country to a liability of $53 million.

The argument against mobile hospitals was compelling and ranged from the poor state of Zambia's roads outside the main urban centres, to the lack of sustainability of the vehicles. Furthermore the public could not help but observe that the money would have been better spent supporting the country's flying doctor service or even existing clinics and hospitals. The government responded to these criticisms either disdainfully or with indifference. Indeed at one point the president took the view that the decision by his government to procure the outdated mobile hospitals from China was not a concern of the citizens.

As the Zambian winter was coming to a close the consensus in the country was that illegal commissions had been paid to highly placed individuals as a result of this procurement. In this regard the government's decision to suddenly call for the repeal of the offence of abuse of office did not help matters. The change in the law would be necessary to facilitate avoidance of criminal prosecution in connection with the mobile hospital loan and other abuses of international aid, should the Banda government lose the 2011 election. By the end of the year the offence of abuse of office had been duly removed from the statute books.

Abuses such as these occur because aid money is easier to steal than taxpayer money. Those who steal aid money do not have an electorate to answer to. Indeed donors of the money are often entirely reliant on the same people who misappropriate the money for the disbursement of the funds.

That is not to say tax dollars are never stolen or misused; they are. The point here is that systemic aid provides an opportunity for embezzlement without accountability to tax payers who generally do not see aid money as their money. In the case of the mobile hospitals, the government itself clearly saw the matter as a private arrangement between itself and the leadership of the People's Republic of China.

Aid and national self esteem

Theft of public money, whether in the form of aid or tax revenue, is obviously injurious to Zambia as it takes away resources from citizens, especially the most vulnerable of them. What is less obvious is the impact of aid on the psyche of the nation.

There is ample evidence that since the 1970s when Zambia first turned to donors for systemic aid, the country has become unhealthily dependent on aid at the expense of national pride and local enterprise. An entire generation of Zambians knows nothing but dependency on aid. On the basis of the evidence they see, this generation generally assumes that Zambians are not capable of paying their way. The monuments of development most visible to this generation were all erected either by foreigners or built by Zambians with foreign money and or technical assistance. The impressive Sion Lumpa church built in the Northern Province entirely by Zambians, most of them women, a half century ago would probably not be built today without a battery of foreign advisers and 'experts'.

On a number of occasions I have made suggestions to different Zambian governments about increasing employment in the country and raising standards of living. Each proposal has invariably elicited the question: 'What will the donors think?' Zambians rarely have the confidence to take the initiative in matters affecting their country's economic development. Equally, Zambians seldom look inward for solutions to their problems.

A European friend employed by the World Bank once asked me how Zambia with its highly intelligent population could be so underdeveloped. The question was legitimate. My convoluted answer pointed to aid and the culture of dependency which has developed since the 1970s as the main culprits.

Donors generally mean well, although, as John Perkins illustrates in *Confessions of an Economic Hit Man*, they can sometimes deliberately lend money to countries knowing full well the countries' inability to pay back the loans. The purpose of the lending in this case is to bankrupt the 'beneficiary' country and make it beholden to the donor country. Even when donors genuinely want a country to develop however, systemic aid tends to do the opposite of what was intended. One of the reasons for this is that aid routinely disbursed by rich countries to poor countries kills local enterprise, reduces the number of people able to pay their way, and eventually creates a nation of beggars with little or no self esteem.

The danger was realised in Eritrea in 1997. I was head of Oxfam Canada when Eritrea announced that it was no longer going to accept international aid and consequently intended to close aid offices including the Oxfam Canada office. There were other Oxfams active in Eritrea so Oxfam International took an interest in the issue. At the Oxfam International meeting in the Hague following Eritrea's declaration, it was decided that Stephan de Clerk, the head of Oxfam Belgium and I should travel to Eritrea on a fact finding mission and then formulate Oxfam International's response.

It so happened that de Clerk and I were both enthusiastic about self reliance and thought Eritrea should be supported in its desire to be more independent of donors. The Eritrean officials we met immediately changed their stance from aggression to cooperation and civility when they found out what our personal positions were. Ms Tesfamichael, the leader of the group we met at the Eritrean Development Agency, took the opportunity to explain why the policy of self reliance had been adopted. I have always remembered vividly her description of aid as an "unhealthy relationship with roots in slavery and subsequently in colonialism."

She then went on to describe how quickly people can make the transition from dignified and hopeful to helpless and dependent. She did so by describing two famine inducing droughts she had witnessed in her country. There was no international aid given with respect to the first drought, but according to Ms Tesfamichael, the population "somehow managed" through their own efforts. Not so with respect to the second drought, that was followed by huge amounts of aid from abroad. On this occasion Ms Tesfamichael was shocked to see wealthy businesspeople lining up to receive free food!

There is a place of course for emergency relief and it may be a mistake to treat this in the same fashion as systemic aid which typically involves routine transfers of resources from rich countries to poor ones, whether or not the poor country in question is facing a natural disaster or some other emergency. Nevertheless, Ms Tesfamichael's example provides food for thought. If businesspeople can quickly suspend their entrepreneurial instincts and pride for a chance to access one-off aid, how much more are they likely to do this when aid is guaranteed on a quotidian basis?

It surely must follow that those who routinely rely on aid as a significant source of income abandon a certain amount of personal responsibility for their well being. It must also be true that the more reliant on foreign assistance countries are, the less responsibility they take for their development. Equally countries that barely control their development agenda will be ill-equipped, materially and intellectually, to contribute to global development.

Indeed, aid-dependent countries are looked upon globally with the same patronising pity that poor people are subjected to domestically. In a documentary done for the Canadian International Development Agency in the late 1980s, a CIDA worker based in Zambia explained to the reporter that he treated Zambians like children because "they are children" dependent on the wisdom and expertise of foreigners like him. This must be an easy conclusion for a person without the necessary historical context and intellectual rigour, to reach. The author of the statement did not know any black Zambians on a social level although he had encountered Zambian university graduates in the course of his work, and he described these people as "not at all like Africans!" All that this person saw was a country unable to pay its way and dependent on foreign largesse for its survival.

Many Zambians would see things in the same light and conclude that their country has nothing to contribute and is therefore not a worthy member of the international community. They would then extrapolate this to their individual circumstances and conclude that they are less worthy than nationals of other countries, certainly less worthy than nationals of countries that provide aid to Zambia. Thus Zambia's dependency on aid would have the same psychological effects on the citizen's mind as colonialism had. This is perhaps what prompted Ms Tesfamichael to describe the relationship between international givers and receivers of aid as rooted in slavery and colonialism.

Aid does indeed appear to give licence to donors to disrespect recipient countries. Even a casual glance at Zambia's newspapers reveals the unhealthy degree to which donor countries with missions in Lusaka involve themselves in what would normally be seen as the country's domestic affairs. For Zambia, the concept of sovereignty is non-existent. From time to time the Zambian political leadership will complain about interference in their internal affairs. That 'interference' however is understandable for as long as Zambia depends on foreign powers to finance its budget. If Zambia wants to be more independent of donors, it must become a contributing player on the global stage. That would start with ending dependency on foreign aid. Weaning Zambia off aid, while potentially painful in the very short term, is unlikely to have deleterious long-term effects. On the contrary, its long term effects would be positive for individual Zambians and the nation as a whole.

The evidence suggests strongly that systemic aid does not support development anyway. If it did, the $1 trillion in aid received by the African continent over the last half-century would have translated into high levels of sustainable prosperity. It has not. On the contrary, "Between 1970 and 1998, when aid flows to Africa were at their peak, poverty in Africa rose from 11 per cent to a staggering 66 per cent." This was the finding of Dambisa Moyo, the Zambian-born economist who has criticised systemic aid. Although the continent does now appear to be making progress, that progress comes largely as a result of trade, and other non-aid initiatives.

On September 02, 2010 when the World Bank vice-president Obiageli Ezekwesili spoke at the inaugural Africa-Singapore Business Forum, he observed that the much maligned continent was turning the corner economically. He talked enthusiastically about Africa being at "about the same point now as where India was 20 years ago and where China was 30 years ago, just before their economic booms set in."

The international banker could not help but recall that ten years earlier the respected *Economist*, echoing harsh sentiments of the time, had dubbed Africa 'The Hopeless Continent.' But this year, *The Economist* in recognition of the huge dividends that Africa is reaping after some tough choices such as mobilising domestic resources, redirecting wasteful spending, investing in basic education and health, reforming public utilities and reducing protectionist policies, has named Africa the 'economic lion' ready to take its place beside the Chinese dragon and the Indian tiger.

It is clear from the speech that this success is not a result of aid but rather the consequence of market-based reform and encouragement of good governance and local entrepreneurship.

Aid, inflation, and exports

International aid typically consists of the provision of value-inflated foreign goods and services, and sometimes cash. Since these goods and services are neither Zambian nor produced or procured after normal Zambian commercial activity, they have the potential to distort the domestic economy. For example, money suddenly introduced into the economy as aid will exaggerate local spending power and fuel inflation. That money would have been introduced into the economy without a corresponding increase in domestic output. Similarly goods brought into the economy will typically be cheaper than locally produced items, and have the effect of driving local producers out of business.

Because of the distortions brought on by aid, few Zambians are able to predict inflationary and currency trends in the country. In a country that produces only a limited number of consumables, the price of goods and services will almost always be affected by sudden injections of cash from abroad. This will be particularly so when that cash ends up in the pockets of individuals who are now able to accelerate their rate of consumption and acquire goods whose purchase they would ordinarily have postponed or had to save for, or maybe even done without. But the sudden cash in their hands will now make it possible for these individuals to spend immediately, leading to price increases, and making the goods unaffordable for the less fortunate who may truly be in need but who have no access to the foreign money fuelling price increases. Depending on the volume of money introduced like this into the economy, the ensuing inflation will almost always require strict monetary policy of high interest rates to soak up the excess liquidity.

That strategy is fine as a way of containing inflation, but in a country like Zambia with vast potential for development and therefore a huge need for investment, high interest rates make investment impossible for small and medium scale businesspeople and difficult even for large operators. Overall therefore there is a decline in investment and consequently a drop in levels of employment. Put differently, the rates of poverty go up as entrepreneurs are denied money for investment.

A similar phenomenon occurs with respect to the exchange rate which is determined almost entirely by Zambia's ability to sell primary commodities like copper, which accounts for 60 per cent of the country's foreign exchange earnings. When copper export earnings climb, as they did in the fourth quarter of 2009 when the commodity brought in over $984 million - compared to $667 million the previous year - the Zambian Kwacha strengthens. A huge portion of these earnings of course goes toward salaries, and maintenance of equipment at the mines. A smaller portion goes toward payment of dividends to foreign based shareholders. And of course the exchequer makes its claim.

The relationship between injection of aid money into the Zambian economy and the appreciation of the Kwacha is even more marked because aid money is entirely from outside the country. Its effect, after being converted into local currency, is to strengthen the Kwacha artificially.

The effect of an artificially strong Kwacha is to make non traditional exports, mostly in tourism and agriculture, very expensive. The consequence of expensive Zambian exports is reduced demand for these goods and services and finally the curtailing of production and disengagement of staff. This again increases poverty which ironically Zambia instinctively seeks to address by appealing for more aid!

A new engagement with the international community

The promise of 1964 was that Northern Rhodesia would be transformed into an independent and sovereign republic that was an equal partner on the international stage. Zambia cannot be such a partner for as long as it is dependent on foreign largesse for its survival. The aid that Zambia has made itself dependent on has not only led to reduced pride in the population, increased corruption, and the undermining of the entrepreneurial spirit, but it has guaranteed Zambia's inability to be self reliant. A new way must therefore be found for Zambia. The country must move from international aid to international cooperation. An example of healthy international cooperation would be Zambian engineers and scientists working with say Japanese car makers to design a car that uses solar power as energy for the air conditioning systems. Another example might involve a Zambian company and a German company agreeing to build a toll highway connecting Livingstone and Chililabombwe.

In both these examples, Zambia would be working with another country for the mutual benefits of the two countries. Both countries would bring something valuable to the table and neither would be subservient to the other.

In this new world however Zambia must fight for a freer global trading system, as it simultaneously develops its domestic economy. Zambia simply must increase goods and services produced in the country and then offer those goods and services not consumed at home, to foreigners.

Zambia's ability to export is currently hindered by the practices of high-income countries.

For example, members of the Organisation for Economic Cooperation and Development subsidise their farmers so heavily that Zambian farm produce has no chance of competing with say European Union agricultural produce. If OECD countries abolished agricultural subsidies and allowed developing countries free access to their markets, the developing countries would earn three times what they currently receive in aid from the OECD members. Patrick Aseah, author of the United Nation's Fourth Economic Report for Africa has shown that elimination of all tariff and non-tariff barriers could result in static gains for developing countries of around $182 billion in services; $162 billion in manufactured goods; and $32 billion, in agriculture.

Zambia should be in the forefront of advocating freer trade, especially with countries that profess to believe in free enterprise. A disavowal of systemic aid and promotion of fair international trade should be part of every Zambian diplomat's brief.

President Mwanawasa appears to have understood the point as the *Marshall Margolis* initiative suggests. In the late 1990s the Toronto-based international lawyer, Marshall Margolis, who, with me, had previously attempted to establish an international arbitration centre in Lusaka, renewed his interest in Zambia.

Marshall and I had discussed the possibility of Zambia and Canada entering into a free trade agreement. The idea was to use the free trade agreement as a means of increasing Zambia's exports to Canada and narrowing the technological gap between the two countries. In the event of a free trade agreement being concluded, Marshall and I planned to persuade a Canadian computer manufacturing company to relocate to Zambia and assemble its computers from there. A company was actually identified and according to our calculations, Zambia would have been able to manufacture high quality computers in either Ndola or Lusaka for a fraction of the Canadian cost. These computers would then be exported to Canada duty free and retail for significantly less than Canadian-made units.

Initial discussion with the Canadian Ministry of External Affairs revealed support for the idea.

Marshall agreed with me that the project was more likely to succeed if he actually became Zambia's honorary consul in Canada, based in Toronto, and led negotiations in that capacity. This was necessary because at the time Zambia had withdrawn its mission to Canada for financial reasons.

Following our previous experience with the proposed arbitration centre, we suspected that Zambian politicians would be the stumbling block to this new project. But President Mwanawasa responded favourably to the first letter I wrote to him on the matter and arranged for Marshall and me to meet him in New York when he attended the United Nations General Assembly in early 2002. We met the president and enjoyed our conversation with him.

Marshall's appointment as honorary consul was eventually made after what seemed like a lifetime. Several opportunities were of course missed as bureaucrats took their time in finalising this very important matter. But this delay was nothing compared to what took place after Marshall asked for a written mandate and a budget (of less than $40,000 per annum) to run the consulate. The delay was compounded by the fact that the only civil servant with enthusiasm about the idea retired from public service. Eventually Marshall Margolis was diagnosed with cancer and died before he could get his mandate and his budget. He had waited for almost two years!

Zambia should continue to seek opportunities like this, but also advocate more trade within the continent, and certainly within Southern Africa, its region. Zambia must use the various regional bodies it belongs to, like the Common Market for Eastern and Southern Africa (COMESA), the Southern African Development Community (SADC), and even the African Union, to encourage trade among African countries.

The high tariffs that African countries impose on each other's goods and services are a hindrance to general African prosperity.

So, Zambia must move from aid dependency to trade and in so doing encourage the international community to be more committed to freer and fairer trade. But in order to maximise the benefits of trade, Zambia also needs to develop a robust domestic economy that will guarantee the country's place as a serious player on the world market. The next two chapters examine some of the things that might be done in order to create a robust domestic economy.

CHAPTER 9

Education: the critical precondition to creating an economy for Zambians

The Zambian economy is both under-regulated and over-regulated, with both phenomena conspiring to undermine the growth of the domestic economy. We saw earlier how the failure to enforce zoning laws has led to a mushrooming of illegal businesses whose impact on the overall economy is to undermine legitimate businesses and make it harder for them to make profits which could be invested for the greater good. But Zambia is also over-regulated in that it is harder to operate a legitimate business in the country than it should be. The point becomes all the more poignant when Zambia is compared to the most successful economies in the world.

The World Bank's Ease of Doing Business project ranks 183 countries on their ease of doing business. A high ranking on the ease of doing business index means the country's regulatory environment is conducive to the operation of business. This index averages the country's percentile rankings on 10 topics: ease of starting a business, dealing with construction permits, employing workers, registering property, getting credit, protecting investors, paying taxes, trading across borders, enforcing contracts, and closing a business.

The rankings from the *Doing Business 2010* report, covering the period June 2008 to May 2009, show that Zambia's overall ranking has improved on the previous year. Even so, the country's ranking at 90 out of 183 suggests that a huge amount of work needs to be done if Zambia is to create a competitive environment for business and realise its economic potential. It is encouraging that in the categories of getting credit and employing workers, Zambia has made significant progress, jumping 38 and 13 places respectively. Zambia is at number 30 with respect to ease of getting credit but only at number 116 with respect to employing workers.

In comparing 2009 to 2010, marginal progress was also made with respect to ease of enforcing contracts and ease of paying taxes, where the country jumped one and three places respectively. Zambia is at number 36 with respect to enforcing contracts but only at number 87 with respect to paying taxes. It remained at the same ranking of number 94 with respect to ease of registering property. Zambia's ranking in all other categories dropped, with the largest drop being in ease of starting a business, from number 72 to 94.

That drop is ominous because the informal sector which has shown so much ingenuity needs to be encouraged to formalise its operations with a view to targeting its local products at the existing middle class, which in turn will expand by creating better paying jobs. In order to do this however the informal sector will have to be regulated with respect not only to places of operation but also with respect to health and safety standards. It is also obvious that the goods and services produced by this sector must be properly packaged and marketed in order to be attractive to the middle class. Zambia's informal sector produces many goods and services ranging from food to furniture to containers etc. These goods and services are generally found unattractive by the middle class because they are not properly packaged and do not carry guarantees concerning health and safety. The legal regime exists to regulate this output but Zambia has invested very little over the past 30 years in the enforcement of regulations pertaining to health, safety, and other standards.

That must change immediately. Zambia needs to enforce all laws and regulations so that businesses operate only in prescribed areas, and the goods produced by these businesses and sold to the public are suitable for consumption by the Zambian middle class (and indeed everyone else) and produced and marketed in compliance with the country's health and safety regulations.

There must be a concerted effort to ensure that all businesses operating in Zambia are registered. There are advantages to registration for both the businessperson and the country.

By registering a business, the entrepreneur signals to the world at large that he or she is available to do business and is prepared to operate in accordance with the country's laws. This in itself gives confidence to would-be customers that their dealings with the business person would be legitimate. Furthermore a registered business is more likely to benefit from business incentives from the government, than an unregistered operation.

A good example of this comes from Canada. In 2009 the government introduced the Home Renovation Tax Credit which allowed homeowners to claim the cost of home improvements up to a maximum of $1,350. As well as encouraging homeowners to renovate their dwellings, this tax credit also generated millions of dollars in additional revenue to the exchequer, as previously unregistered contractors quickly formalised their operations in order to take advantage of increased business in the sector. Customers wishing to take advantage of the tax credit only engaged duly registered contractors able to issue verifiable receipts.

It is easier to collect taxes from registered businesses than unregistered ones. It is also easier for the government to enforce good business practices and health and safety regulations in the formal sector than the informal sector, where most unregistered businesses are found.

Given these advantages, it is imperative that Zambia makes every effort to reduce further the time required to launch a business as well as the cost of doing so.

Progress has already been made with the number of procedures necessary to start a business. The Doing Business 2010 report shows that there are six steps to be taken before a business can be launched. The number of steps for Sub-Saharan Africa is 9.4, while the number for the OECD countries is 5.7. There is not much difference between Zambia and the OECD average with respect to this particular indicator, but the gap grows significantly with respect to time required to launch a business and the cost of launching the business. The time required in Zambia is 18 days compared to 13 days in the OECD. The cost of launching a business is 28.4 per cent of income per capita in Zambia, compared to 4.7 per cent of income per capita in the OECD.

Improving the ease with which businesses are launched is only one step however on the road to creation of a robust domestic economy. In the longer term the sustainability of the domestic economy will depend on Zambia's ability to keep its population skilled and educated. In this regard the education process should start very early in the lives of Zambians. The correlation between national academic and skill levels on the one hand, and domestic prosperity on the other, is well known. What is perhaps less well known is the connection between government procurement policies and domestic wealth. This chapter will propose concrete ways in which the Zambian government can increase the wealth of Zambians through procurement. But first, we shall examine the importance of education in Zambia's economic future.

The value of Education

Many of the challenges facing Zambia could be overcome through a comprehensive education system that had the effect of increasing many times over the individual capacity of nationals. The evidence is overwhelming that education has a hugely positive impact on society. The difference between an educated person and an uneducated one is that the former is trained to think and take responsible decision. Thus education has the effect of maximising rational behaviour in human beings.

The internet has made it possible to transmit huge amounts of knowledge and information across the globe instantaneously. But with only five per cent of the population able to access the internet, many Zambians continue to live in ignorance and consequently continue to underperform. With basic adult literacy at 68 per cent and many schools unable to offer an adequate education, too many Zambians remain uneducated and therefore unable to take advantage of knowledge and wisdom easily obtainable from the internet. The internet has in fact increased the gap between the educated and the uneducated because the educated person can now get even more information, even more quickly.

Zambia must open the window to knowledge for all nationals. Individual Zambians constitute the nation's most important resource. It follows that education must be available to every individual if Zambia is to achieve sustainable growth and development.

It is no accident that the most successful economies in the world have very high literacy rates.

Barbados, a country less well endowed than Zambia in terms of natural resources, has a literacy rate of 99.7 per cent. The country's GDP per capita income at $19,300 is twenty times that of Zambia's. Bermuda, another country with fewer natural resources than Zambia, has a literacy rate of 98 per cent and a GDP per capita income in excess of $69,000.

The performance of countries like Barbados and Bermuda, founded by descendants of West African slaves, shows that the negative aspects of colonialism from which Zambia continues to suffer can be overcome.

Educating Zambia

The formal learning journey for Zambians must start as early as possible, especially given the paucity of good child care facilities in the country. Zambia must aim to have all children from the age of four in full day learning programmes. Investing in the education of young Zambians in this way would give the children a firm foundation for success in life and have long-term benefits for the entire economy. Thus children would be given the opportunity to develop inter-personal skills and learn to manage diversity and differences of opinion early in life. They would also be exposed to rational thinking early so that by the time they reached adulthood rational analysis would be second nature to them. In a young country, getting the youngest citizens in a learning environment early, also promotes national awareness, and national pride.

Clearly, these schools must be well equipped and well run, sending the message always that Zambia's young people are the country's most valuable resource. The country must resolutely refuse to believe the myth that Zambia cannot afford to provide its population with a good education for the benefit of the individuals concerned as well as for the benefit of the country. We saw earlier that Zambia loses about US$70,000,000 each year through misappropriation and mismanagement. If that money were diverted to education, it would go a long way toward guaranteeing a good education for the country's young people.

The reader may also recall that according to Lynn Cole, the head of the Illinois based non governmental organisation RISE International, a school can actually be built for as little as $12,000. So, if all the money lost through corruption were used for educational purposes instead, Zambia would be in a position to build at least 5,833 schools each year. Of course the country would not need to build that number of schools each year, nor would the country wish to restrict itself to the Cole model in the construction of these schools, but the point debunks the myth that Zambia is too poor to provide the necessary education to its population. Indeed the debate on learning should not be dominated by discussion of the cost to the treasury of good education. The evidence from around the world is that education can never be more expensive than the lack of it.

It is therefore a national disgrace that in 2008 there were 800,000 Zambian children who could not attend formal education because they lived too far from a school or came from families that were too poor to pay for the most basic of requirements for school going children.

A number of NGOs and the Zambian government have been active in constructing schools over the past few years. It will however take a while before they can be ready to absorb all children currently unable to attend school. But Zambia does not have to wait for completion of the construction programme before extending child enrolment. There is something the Zambian government can do in the intervening period to address the shortage of places for so many school age children.

At any one time there are thousands of young people who are unable to proceed to higher education or get a job despite having a secondary school certificate. Many of these youngsters live with working parents who are away from the family home during business hours. The unemployed school leavers are typically left at home with nothing meaningful to do.

Both the children and the homes could be turned into educational resources with beneficial effects for the country. Let's assume there were 10,000 school leavers without jobs or immediate prospects of entry into institutions of higher learning.

As part of its plan to increase access to primary school education, the government could invite these young people to attend intensive teaching courses for a period of say three months. The young people would already know the substance of the subjects they learnt at secondary school and the purpose of the courses would be to teach them basic aspects of teaching. The school leavers would then be invited to assume responsibility for the education of three children each, in their homes. The teaching would of course take place during working hours when there was minimal traffic and noise in the house. This could be done in the sitting room or even in the grounds. The newly minted teachers would be engaged as independent contractors, but required to follow the national curriculum, in addition to providing a meal to their pupils, and basic materials.

If each new teacher were to take three students, a total of 30,000 children would immediately have access to primary school education. All this would be done without investing a single cent in a new building! Since the new teachers would be engaged as independent contractors, the government's obligation would be to pay them a monthly fee, and ensure that they were following the national curriculum and feeding the children, as agreed to in a contract. Random inspections by the ministry of education would be necessary to ensure the continuing suitability of premises and compliance with the teaching contract.

The cost of this arrangement, which provides badly needed employment to otherwise unemployed school leavers while educating the nation's youngest citizens, would be comparatively small. A secondary school teacher earns about $300 per month. If that same amount were to be paid to the teachers under the home schooling plan, the total annual bill would be $3 million. This is not a large amount given the importance of education and in light of other expenditures the Zambian government is prepared to incur on doubtful priorities.

In November 2008, the Zambian government introduced three bills aimed at increasing salaries and improving conditions of service for constitutional office holders including the president, the vice president, and cabinet ministers. The increase raised eyebrows as at that time Zambia was experiencing an economic recession and most prudent people considered the increase in pay for some of the country's wealthiest citizens, unnecessary. Some pointed to the more responsible behaviour of one mining company which reduced the pay of senior executives by 25 per cent, as the example the Zambian government should follow.

The advice was not taken. Far from it, the government backdated the pay increase to January 2008. In addition to this increase, the 2010 budget included an item of $13.3 million for mid term gratuity for members of parliament, including all cabinet ministers. Each MP's entitlement under the gratuity scheme is $84,000, an amount equal to the monthly salary of 280 secondary school teachers!

The mining company that slashed executive pay during the recession did so in order to reduce redundancies among miners and also to help maintain social services to its work force during a time of financial constraint. It is not unreasonable to ask public officials in Zambia to become less avaricious in order to reduce the likelihood of children not attending school and also to help maintain high quality education.

Continuing Education

The Times Higher Education World University Rankings rate universities on the quality of education they offer. The rankings provide broad comparative performance information. They are helpful not only to parents anxious to send children to good universities, but also to countries and academic institutions looking for collaborative ventures, especially in research and development. Good universities are rightly seen as essential to the growth of a dynamic and competitive 21st century economy. It is therefore regrettable that none of the Zambian universities claim a spot on the current table of 200 universities. The University of Zambia does however feature on the 2010 World University Ranking for Africa where it is ranked 23 out of 100.

In order to improve their performance and ability to attract good students, Zambian universities must base their admissions strictly on merit and be properly resourced. While the bulk of the funding will continue to come from the state, society as a whole must be prepared to pay higher fees, and alumni must also be more willing to make contributions aimed at advancing higher education at their old universities.

In 2009 tuition and accommodation fees for Arts students at the University of Zambia were a paltry $858 per semester. The figure for science students was $1,034. These rates of fees are unlikely to provide an adequate funding base for a university aspiring to be a world class centre of learning. Low fees combined with willingness by university authorities to lower admission standards for unqualified but favoured applicants have led to corruption in admissions and overcrowding in both residences and class rooms. The result of all this has been a decline in the overall standards of a once superior institution. Zambia has little chance of realising her potential if education is not treated as a priority. Both the state and society must be prepared to pay the necessary price to ensure that the country has first rate institutions of higher learning.

But charging realistic fees should not result in talented young men and women from low income families being denied places at colleges or universities.

To avoid this, the state must create a merit-based scholarship scheme for the brightest students. Government incentives for private enterprises to support students must also be put in place.

The fees from 2009 suggest that it is more expensive for students to study sciences and medicine at the University of Zambia, than general arts. In fact the Zambian economy would benefit more if science studies were more accessible than arts studies.

The emergence of both India and China as economic giants was preceded by heavy investment in science education. A 2009 study by Ernst and Young and the Associated Chambers of Commerce and Industry showed that India has outperformed the US, Europe and Japan in numbers of students graduating in Mathematics and Science. Furthermore, India has the second largest pool of scientists and engineers in the world.

According to DS Rawat, the secretary general of the Associated Chambers of Commerce and Industry, India produces 690,000 students of science every year. Its closest rival is China which produces 530,000 such graduates each year. The respective figures for Japan, the United States, and the European Union are 350,000, 420,000 and 470,000.

Zambia is a smaller country that cannot of course produce this number of graduates in any field of education. The country can and must however increase drastically the proportion of science and mathematics graduates it produces. This can be done by introducing a graduated science scholarship which would virtually guarantee financial support for every qualified applicant wishing to study science and mathematics at university. The extent of the financial support would depend on the student's performance in the final secondary school examinations, and would reward the brightest students with full scholarships.

Zambia should also set aside some money for post graduate scholarships for exceptional international students.

In keeping with the proposal that the country wean itself off international aid and commit itself instead to the promotion of genuine international cooperation, scholarships for international students should come with a condition requiring the fortunate foreign scholars to teach in Zambian secondary schools. Thus an international student doing a PhD in an aspect of biodiversity would be required to teach biology or a related subject at a Zambian secondary school. Depending on subject matter, some of these students may be assigned to teach undergraduates at the university itself. The idea is for Zambia to foster international academic collaboration and maximise opportunities for the country from such contact.

Post-secondary education should not of course be purely academic. Colleges and other educational institutes should be encouraged to offer vocational training programs apart from regular diploma or certificate studies. Online education such as that offered by the Zambia Open University must also be encouraged to address the educational needs of the working population. Zambia needs to change direction and attain prosperity as soon as possible. This can best be done if there is a realisation that education is for everyone including working people. In addition to acquiring fresh qualifications, working people must have the ability to update and upgrade their knowledge and skill levels for their personal development.

Colleges must also offer opportunities to showcase innate Zambian ingenuity such as that possessed by Charles Mubanga Mumba. The largely self-trained electrical engineer generates power from a small hydro power station using an inexpensive generator, tractor rim and other components at Kapumo falls on Mutotoshi River. Mumba's formal education does not go beyond Grade 11.

Mumba used five drums to create a heavy flow of water necessary for turning the turbines he created from an old tractor rim and other scrap metal. Since 2002 Mumba has routinely generated power for use in his house as well as his mother's home nearby. The project has increased Mumba's confidence and greatly raised his family's standard of living. Mumba is often contracted by government institutions to repair equipment ranging from ultrasound machines to computers to motor vehicles.

The children's life too has changed for the better as availability of electricity has allowed them to study at night, not just during the day.

Mumba was recognized for his ingenuity and contribution to Zambian scientific achievement by President Mwanawasa but despite this and the innovator's stated interest in education, no college in Zambia has thus far seen fit to exploit his immense talent by inviting him to share his knowledge and vocational interests with students, or indeed giving him an opportunity to further his formal education. This extraordinary man has much to contribute in the effort to intellectually emancipate the nation and promote excellence. Educational excellence and equal access to it is essential in the preparation of Zambia for global competitiveness. The country cannot afford anything less than a universal system of excellent education. Without this, Zambia will continue to underperform.

Chapter 10

People's Economy

Through enforcement of by laws and regulations that aid the conduct of orderly business and through practical and people-focused procurement policy, Zambia can create the basis for a dynamic economy. The extent to which the economy grows thereafter will depend to a large extent on Zambia's ability to educate the entire population and maximise the societal benefits we now know arise when a higher percentage of citizens have post- secondary education. For example a 2007 New York College Board study found that higher rates of volunteering, voting and donating blood correspond to higher levels of education as do lower unemployment and poverty rates. Similarly, socially valuable behaviour, such as tolerance for diverse opinion, seems to increase with education as well. The study also found a strong correlation between an educated workforce and higher wages for all.

Obviously more needs to be done to ensure excellent universal education for the entire nation. Even so, there are steps that can be taken now that might result in immediate economic improvement for citizens and set the stage for spectacular growth in the future. In order to do so Zambia must be prepared to challenge many assumptions the country makes about development, and allow the market to signal what people want.

Road Construction

The assumption is almost always made that all road construction requires huge capital outlays and the involvement of large corporations. While this may be true for trunk roads, it is not always true with respect to community roads. Most community roads in Zambia are no more than paths created by sheer usage over time. These paths are in fact a signal from the market that people need a road. They are also an opportunity for construction of community based labour intensive roads.

Consider this example from South Africa. The Amadiba community of Eastern Cape Province was given an opportunity to construct a six-meter wide and forty-kilometer long road that connected the community in OR Tambo District to a trunk road. The immediate effect of constructing the road was to create employment, mostly short term, in a community where 75 per cent of the population was unemployed. About 60 per cent of the newly-employed were women. The road construction uplifted community spirit and generated huge optimism. This is evident from the perceptions that the community recorded about the impact of the project on the quality of life. A subsequent survey by M Mashiri, D Thevadasan, and R Zukulu revealed high levels of satisfaction with the impact of the project on the community. Thus all respondents thought travel to main settlements had improved. No one thought it had deteriorated. Perhaps that is to be expected. Less obvious was the finding that 96.6 per cent of respondents thought local clinic visitation had improved with only 3.4 per cent disagreeing, and 93.1 per cent thought access to community centres had improved while 6.9 per cent disagreed.

In addition to the temporary jobs created, there were also marketable skills developed and some villagers went on to become construction supervisors with an opportunity to obtain permanent employment. Small businesses in the community also reported an increase in trade especially during the construction period. Altogether this remote community saw a decline in poverty rates and an increase in communal capacity.

There are many communities in Zambia that could benefit from labour intensive road construction whose beneficial attributes include cost effectiveness and employment generation. The International Labour Organization estimates that labour intensive road construction is between 10 and 30 per cent cheaper than capital intensive road construction.

Anyone driving on the main road from the Copperbelt to Lusaka will be struck by the number of makeshift markets along the way. These trading centres, which operate illegally, are in fact connected to villages and other communities that produce the items sold there.

Collaboration between communities, local authorities, central government, and the private sector could result in the formalisation of these markets for the benefit of the community and the country.

A number of communities close to the Ndola/Kabwe road would be prime candidates for this proposal. For any of them, the first step might be the construction of a labour intensive road from the supplier communities to the roadside markets. The relatively low cost of construction would be borne by both the local authority and the central government. The signal from the market in this instance is twofold - construction of a road to service the community, and establishment of a well serviced roadside trading post that includes facilities like public toilets and parking space. So, the makeshift market must be replaced by a safe, modern and properly serviced roadside facility. Thus the new market must comply with planning law, in addition to being aesthetically pleasing.

The new roadside market would now be operated by entrepreneurs leasing stalls from the local authority. Community suppliers would sell to regulated traders in the formal sector and expect a fair price for their produce. More travellers would stop over because of increased safety, parking, and public toilets. This would of course increase the likelihood of travellers buying from the market. In these circumstances it would make sense to enforce laws against illegal and nuisance traders in unauthorised areas. The reduction in illegal trading would eliminate unfair competition for legitimate entrepreneurs and increase their profits which in turn would increase the sustainability of revenue to the local authority in the form of fees from the lease of stalls.

The investment originally made in the construction of the road by the local authority would yield a return not only in the form of fees for stalls but possibly also from property taxes payable on the value of privately owned but publicly serviced permanent structures at the roadside market. The return to both the local authority and the central government is the increased wealth in the community as well as the creation of a safer roadside market.

For the private sector, an opportunity to trade fairly and raise capital over the longer term is created.

And of course the community wins in a big way by being able to transport its produce in larger volume to an expanding clientele. Furthermore, the community has access to both short term and longer term employment because even after the labour intensive construction has ended, the new roadside market will require parking attendants, janitors, cleaners etc.

Encouraging communities to build feeder roads for themselves allows large construction companies to concentrate on larger projects such as trunk roads. Typically, the Zambian government turns to donors whenever a need for construction or maintenance of a trunk road is identified. In fact aid is not the only way of constructing trunk roads. The private sector can play a useful role in building the road network that Zambia so badly needs.

In this regard cautious welcome must be given to Finance Minister Situmbeko Musokotwane's announcement in mid 2010 that his government had plans to significantly expand the country's infrastructure by investing in a number of projects including roads, airports, border posts, farming blocks, power generation, transport and housing units. This was going to be done through what he called public private arrangements.

Unfortunately the way these public private arrangements would work was not explained in any detail but a month earlier another cabinet minister explained that the government was waiting for funding. This suggests that the Zambian government plans to fund the development with aid money. There is another way however that would see Zambia construct roads by utilization of international commercial connections, rather than aid.

It is clear to all that the main trunk road connecting Livingstone town in the South to Chililabombwe in the Copperbelt province is no longer adequate for the transportation of people and goods from one end of the country to the other. While traffic has expanded greatly in recent years, the road's capacity to handle more vehicles has not grown.

A business case for the construction of a new dual carriageway from Livingstone to Chililabombwe can be made easily.

Instead of asking for foreign aid to construct the road, the government could post an international tender for the construction of the carriageway as a toll road. The tender would be of interest to companies at home and abroad wishing to invest in Zambia for the longer term. The likely outcome is that a consortium of Zambian and foreign interests would emerge to construct the dual carriageway. Zambia's ability to attract this kind of long term investment would at least in part depend on the country's reputation at the time as a reliable destination of foreign direct investment with a commitment to the rule of law and a credible dispute settlement mechanism. If these conditions are satisfied, Zambia could see the construction of a high quality road completed in short order for the benefit of both the country and the investors.

The building of the road would not however be the end of the story. Opportunities would also be created for Zambian entrepreneurs to start businesses such as filling stations along the new road. The government too would have an opportunity to serve more people through facilities like health and recreation centres for the use of motorists and communities living near the new road.

Local government

The jobs generated by construction of community roads are important but still miniscule compared to the jobs that would be created by the dual carriageway between Livingstone and Chililabombwe. Opportunities for significant job creation would also exist if both levels of government were prepared to be more innovative and to use procurement for this purpose.

The City of Ndola, like other towns on the Copperbelt, has a lovely aerial view suggesting well laid out streets. The reality however is that visitors to the city have great difficulty finding their way around because most streets no longer have name signs. The signs have fallen off and the local authority has done nothing to repair or replace them.

When asked why the city has no signage, the officials' knee jerk response is that there is no money. In fact it is not the lack of money that is responsible for this; it is lack of innovation and a reluctance to think outside the box.

While streets remain unsigned in much of Ndola, the city also boasts some of the best sign makers in the business. The young men engaged in the trade typically serve motorists requiring number plates and road safety triangles. They are lucky to take home $5 after a hard day's work, and often earn less than that. Assuming the council contracted these sign makers to work as independent contractors on two hundred streets for an average fee of $10 per street and assigned one sign maker to work on 10 streets, a total of 20 sign makers would be employed at a cost of $2000. Thereafter the council would call upon the sign makers as the need arose and would use them as part of an overall street maintenance plan. The street sign makers would of course continue to do other work such as car number plate signage, building signage etc. But the fact of being given work by the council, however seasonal, would make the business of sign making more sustainable and have the effect of increasing income in the community.

The cost of $2000 to sort out the street signage problem in Ndola is affordable. In 2009 Ndola City Council had a total income of $6,000,000 in grants from the central government, property taxes and levies. Of this, 21 per cent was spent on service provision, two per cent on infrastructure development, and 77 per cent on recurrent expenditure - mostly in the form of emoluments.

It seems clear from the pattern of expenditure that the council needs to have better priorities. Clearly, the council needs to cut its emoluments bill and use the money to fund services and infrastructure development which will in turn increase job creation in the private sector.

Keeping Ndola clean could also be achieved on the same basis; contract the work out to qualified members of the public and generate jobs in the community.

City Parking is Big Business

Perhaps the best opportunity for generating jobs in Zambia's cities lies in the labour intensive parking system I proposed in 1991. The plan was subsequently shared with Dr Silane Mwenechanya, one of Zambia's leading business and legal consultants, in the mid 1990s. His assessment was that the plan's strength lay in its simplicity. He also made suggestions as to how the plan could be adapted to existing socioeconomic reality.

In early 1991 I was asked to go to Zambia to help the Bank of Zambia, then under the able leadership of Canadian banker Jacques Bussières, to do a study on the development of a viable money market in the country. Bussières was sympathetic to my view that a viable money market could not be developed without the active participation of local authorities, since they were at different times both potential borrowers and potential lenders. But before the creation of any market a way had to be found to increase local governments' ability to increase revenue.

To illustrate how this could be done I looked at ways in which parking in Lusaka could be made profitable for the local authority. Lusaka had 100,000 parking spaces, and I believed the city council should place a value of $1 on each space. The combined potential income of all those places would thus be $100,000 a day. Unlike other parking systems however, no parking meters would be employed.

Instead there would be a parking attendant with responsibility for ten cars. The attendant's responsibility would be to ensure that each parked car had a sticker indicating payment for that day, and the attendant would be authorised to issue the permits. To avoid attendants carrying too much cash, arrangements would be made with a local bank to provide mobile banking services. For every ten attendants there would be an inspector who would manage the front line workers.

The 1991 study suggested that the attendants be paid twice the going rate for security guards employed by diplomatic missions in Zambia. The inspectors would earn twice the pay of attendants. In addition to personnel, the parking system would require a couple of tow trucks and mobile communication devices. Uniforms would be another cost.

Taking all foreseeable expenses into account the study's preliminary finding was that a profit of $5,000,000 per annum was realisable from this venture. We both agreed that the business should not be run by the council but by private concerns. Dr Mwenechanya favoured a system that offered the ten spaces to individual entrepreneurs. I favoured a concession of the whole system to a reputable company chosen after a competitive tender.

We consulted Lusaka City Council as we fine-tuned the proposal. Unfortunately the council had little appreciation of the detail but were seduced by the potential to make money, and in clear violation of intellectual property laws and business ethics, implemented the proposal without our knowledge, hoping to keep the projected $5million profit. Not surprisingly, the scheme failed. The success of the system depended on it being operated in accordance with the principles of market economics, with concomitant discipline. Whether operated by one large company or a number of individual entrepreneurs, Dr Mwenechanya and I had envisaged the operators taking the risk and being rewarded with an annual profit of $5million. The city council would then receive an annual concession fee of $1million per annum, without the headache of running the business.

But the benefit to society as a whole would go beyond the concession fee paid to the council, as 10,000 new jobs for young people would be created. These young people would earn enough to pay council levies and possibly income tax. They would then go on to spend the money they earned and help maintain or create new jobs in the rest of the economy. Furthermore, with each car under the watchful eye of an attendant, security in Lusaka would be greatly improved as car thefts declined.

A decade after my study, the Cape Town adopted a similar system to regulate parking in the central business district.

Kent Morkel, the Council's Executive Committee member responsible for Economic Development, Tourism and Property, welcomed the decision as a major step in the city's drive to provide a safe, clean environment. He saw the system as evidence of how public and private sectors can cooperate for the common good. He also thought well-regulated parking for both residents and tourists helped Cape Town to be globally competitive and attractive to tourists.

Councillor Morkel's reasoning applies to Zambian cities too. The parking system proposed in 1991 should be implemented as soon as possible, with necessary adjustments. If the major Copperbelt towns also adopted the system, the province could easily generate another 10,000 jobs.

Enforcing by laws

But it is not just entrepreneurial ventures like the proposed parking system that are necessary to place Zambia on the path to prosperity. Enforcing council by laws would also help. For example, by laws require all households in municipalities to be well maintained in a hygienic manner. There is even a legal expectation that houses will be painted at frequent intervals. Some by laws actually require home occupants to maintain manicured lawns. If local authorities announced their intention to enforce these by laws and actually demonstrated their willingness to take action against households disregarding the law, a market would soon develop for the provision of gardening and other property maintenance services.

The very nature of the work would ensure that these services were provided by local companies and thus an opportunity would be created to increase community wealth, with the usual multiplier effect in the rest of the economy. Furthermore, local authorities would have to lead by example. They could not reasonably expect householders to obey the law when they themselves did not. So, local governments would have to ensure that areas zoned as parks were not only treated as such but were actually maintained as parks for everyone's enjoyment.

The local authorities may themselves hire contractors to do this work for them. The principle would also apply to maintenance of cemeteries, public buildings, public toilets etc.

The enforcement of by laws has been analysed in the context of economic development. Enforcing laws also has the advantage of creating healthier communities. This is something President Mwanawasa understood. In launching his Keep Zambia Clean and Healthy campaign, Mwanawasa's local government ministry identified many advantages of cleanliness and good hygiene practices in the home, community, and workplace. According to the ministry, the benefits are not only economic but also 'physical and psychological.'

The Secretariat of the Make Zambia Clean and Healthy Programme described the benefits in the launch document as follows:

> Good personal hygiene not only makes us look and feel better about ourselves, it also helps prevent skin infections, scabies, lice, gum and tooth disease and a whole host of other infectious diseases. A clean home and surroundings, where the yard is swept, rubbish removed, and water protected will be a far happier and healthier place for children, than one that is unkempt.
>
> Clean children grow stronger and better than others, they are less likely to be sick, and will do better at school, as they do not miss as many school days and have more energy for their studies. Lack of illness does not only make the home a happier place, it also saves money as there is less expenditure on medicines and parents do not have to take time off to care for sick children.
>
> A clean environment with no rubbish or overgrown grass or ponds of stagnant water means [fewer] mosquitoes, flies, or snakes. Apart from being aesthetically pleasing it also means less malaria, dysentery, cholera and other infectious diseases.
>
> Clean schools with proper ablution blocks for boys and girls, not only allow the next generation to learn good practices, they also keep them healthy. A clean and tidy school environment encourages children to develop tidy practices which when applied to their studies will result in them performing better and achieving higher grades.
>
> A business or workplace with a clean environment achieves many advantages. Not only does it contribute to [a reduction in] employee absence through illness with its negative effect on productivity and business costs, it provides an attractive environment that will make

> staff feel and perform better. Productivity increases and the business benefits.
> In addition, an attractive and clean business environment gives a strong positive signal about its products, to existing and potential clients which can prove to be a significant advantage in a competitive market. It is also known that most people would prefer to enter clean premises which are [well maintained] with an attractive exterior, than one that is untidy, strewn with rubbish, and [smelly].

It is regrettable that no clear leadership on this matter has been shown since the demise of Mr Mwanawasa. We can only hope that the obvious economic benefits derived from enforcement of by laws will lead to an automatic appreciation of broader societal benefits such as better health.

Procurement

The extent to which the political leadership can be sidestepped is unfortunately limited in a country like Zambia with a history of a dominant state. Procurement as a tool for economic regeneration cannot succeed without a conscious effort on the part of the government to increase opportunities for nationals.

As a matter of policy the Zambian government should announce at the earliest opportunity that it will not consume anything that does not have Zambian content.

The business sector should be given a timeframe within which to increase local content in goods and services consumed by the government. This policy need not affect consumption patterns in the private sector - its purpose would be to use government as a vehicle for the promotion of Zambian entrepreneurship.

Let's imagine that on April 1, 2011, the government of Zambia announced that with effect from June the following year it would not ordinarily accept goods and services that did not have local content. The amount of content would depend on the particular item. In the case of motor vehicles, for example, it might suffice, at least in the early years of the policy, to simply assemble the vehicles locally. On the other hand, packaged food consumed by institutions like the army, might need a local content level of say 60 per cent. Products already made in Zambia would of course qualify for purchase and consumption by government.

It is estimated that each year the Zambian government imports about 9,000 vehicles for its various arms. The exact number is difficult to ascertain because many of these vehicles are bought for the intelligence network which is unwilling to divulge its purchases. If Zambia were to announce that these vehicles would have to be assembled in Zambia, and that in future they would be required to have a certain amount of local content, well before the deadline of June 1, 2012, the country would be inundated with offers of vehicle manufacturers wanting to 'corner' the Zambian market. The car makers' hope would be to sell cars to the broader national and regional market, using the guaranteed 9,000 vehicles as a starting point.

The proper way to determine who eventually is allowed to set up the assembly plant would be by way of public tender with the process stipulating the conditions of maximum employment for Zambians, and a commitment to use Zambian-made products in the manufacturing process as soon as possible.

The extent to which the assembly plant is automated would depend on a combination of factors including the preferences of the investor.

In general however, a modern highly automated plant requires an average of three people to produce one car. So, even if our assembly plant was unable to supply the general public and regional consumers, some 27,000 Zambians would secure employment. The number of employees would be even higher if the plant was less automated but we shall assume our plant is as automated as the average North American plant.

Ray Tanguay, President of Toyota Motor Manufacturing Canada, has estimated that for every job created in the car industry, between five and seven jobs are created in the broader economy. Conservatively then it can be estimated that a policy on the part of the government to only buy motor vehicles assembled in Zambia would result not only in the direct employment of 27,000 Zambians, but would also result in 135,000 jobs being created in the broader economy. In reality the figure would be even more impressive because the vehicles assembled locally would be purchased by the Zambian private sector too and possibly other consumers in the Southern African region, which would all add to demand for labour in the industry.

The multiplier effect in the motor vehicle industry is not unique to North America. It is a phenomenon that is considered a given in Europe where the automotive industry is seen as the 'engine' of the economy, with one in ten jobs dependent directly or indirectly on the automotive sector. According to the European Automobile Manufacturers Association the industry is also the largest investor in innovation and research and development and of course the driver of European exports. When it is performing well, the industry has a huge positive impact on the wider economy because of the thousands of small and medium sized companies involved in the supply chain, vehicle sales and after-sales services.

Zambia could, by intelligent use of the procurement process, develop a healthy automotive industry with a clear role to play in the effort of leading the country to sustainable prosperity. The automotive industry, reliant as it is on successful research and development could also contribute to establishment of excellence in institutions of higher learning.

Government institutions can also be used for the purpose of encouraging the development of more basic skills. For example, there appears to be a surprisingly large number of underemployed but competent tailors in most Zambian townships and even some villages. Subject to compliance with the established standard, these tailors should be given the opportunity to compete for contracts for the manufacture of uniforms for soldiers and other public officers. According to published figures, the Zambian armed forces have a personnel of 22,000. If on average it costs $100 a year to properly clothe each member of the armed forces, then there is two million dollars' worth of work that could be given to tailors across Zambia. This money would go directly into communities and have a huge multiplier effect.

And this exercise should not be confined to military or police attire. Institutions like the army, air force, police service, prisons, and schools are all potentially big consumers of packaged food. At the moment they consume far less than they could as our story from the Lusaka Central Prison illustrates. This is because Zambia has not done a good job of preserving the food it produces.

I remember once driving from Chingola to Lusaka during a time of drought. Even at this time however I noticed mountains of both sweet and Irish potatoes at makeshift markets. So abandunt was the produce that one could have assumed that the much discussed drought may have been a figment of official imagination. In fact the drought was real but the shortage of rain was concentrated in the Southern Province, the traditional leader in maize production. Had Zambia invested in a viable food transportation and preservation system, the drought would not have had the impact it had because the country would have been able to transport food from the surplus areas to the defict areas, and would also have been able to preserve that food for consuption in the post harvest months.

Food preservation would be aided by an invitation to Zambian entrepreneurs to participate in public tenders for the provision of food to government institutions. Knowing that they had a ready market, entrepreneurs would find a way of preserving food for distribution and sale throughout the year.

This would end the frequent sad phenomena of food wastage during harvest times and food shortages for the rest of the year.

Another area that requires immediate government direction is the furniture industry. Visitors to Zambia are surprised at the quality of furniture made by craftspeople without much formal training. There are also of course other woodworkers who are less skilled but whose products are still on sale because the government has not enforced laws on the quality of manufactured furniture. This industry has potential for growth and the government should regulate it with a view to guaranteeing quality and formalising the furniture business.

The first step perhaps is to enforce by laws that prohibit roadside trading which is where most of the furniture business in Zambia is currently conducted. This should be followed by an offer of space for the sale of furniture at designated premises zoned for commercial use. As long as the government and local authorities enforce the law relating to zoning and commerce, legitimate furniture manufacturers will move to the right areas for business, knowing that illegitimate traders will not be permitted to have an unfair advantage by plying their trade illegally.

Once by laws and zoning regulations have been enforced, the government should establish quality standards for the industry and make it mandatory for industry participants to follow these standards.

Critically the government should then undertake only to buy furniture made locally and in accordance with established quality standards. In this way, court house furniture, school desks, home furniture for government officials, furniture in police stations, furniture in security service offices, and anywhere else the government is obliged to furnish, would be made locally. Of course in order to supply this furniture, the manufacturer and seller would be registered as business entities and therefore liable for tax. The decision to get furniture from local producers would not only raise incomes and fortify the Zambian middle class, it would also increase revenue to the exchequer, without raising tax rates.

A people's tourist sector

Expanding the Zambian middle class would also have the effect of increasing demand for services such as those provided by the tourist industry. Previously, tourism has been seen essentially as a service for foreigners. In the new Zambia tourism should be seen as a service as much for local people as for foreigners. This should be reflected in both the provision and consumption of tourist services.

It has to be said again that Zambia has lost many opportunities in this regard. While the country has world class resorts such as the hotels in Livingstone, these facilities cater mostly to foreigners. Increasing the size of the Zambian middle class will necessarily increase the number of Zambian tourists making use of these facilities. But all tourists need more choice than what is currently on offer. There are relatively inexpensive ways of expanding choice for both locals and foreigners.

A visitor to the Livingstone Railway Museum will be impressed with the official guide's knowledge of the history of railways. The visitor will also be saddened by the dilapidated state of the two railway passenger coaches on display. The wooden floors of the coaches have largely been eaten away by termites and are liable to collapse, so the few visitors who go to the museum have to tread carefully as the staff hope that no expensive lawsuit will arise from their employer's negligence. The work needed to restore these lovely coaches can be performed by the nearby Livingstone Trades Training Institute. The request has never been made however because the museum has never felt able to pay for the repairs. It certainly cannot raise enough money from the fee of around one dollar charged for entry to the site.

The museum is in fact a potential financial success. There are clubs for railway enthusiasts all over the world, including in the United Kingdom, United States, Canada, Australia, New Zealand and India. Although there are railway enthusiasts in Zambia they do not yet appear to have formed themselves into a club.

The Livingstone Railway Museum would be a delight for the tens of thousands of steam train enthusiasts who belong to these organisations, and be a welcome opportunity for Zambians with similar interests. The museum not only houses an exhibit of memorabilia and photographs of the early days in Livingstone, it is also home to nineteenth century steam locomotives, and those vintage railway coaches. But unlike the coaches, the steam locomotives seem to be in reasonably good shape.

The coaches could be refurbished however and turned into theme and period accommodation for tourists with a particular interest in railways. Assuming two refurbished coaches comfortably accommodated twenty tourists, even a relatively small tariff of $50 a night would contribute significantly to the earnings of the Livingstone Railway Museum. Medium cost hotels in Livingstone are scarce and consequently have a high occupancy rate. Assuming a relatively low occupancy rate of eighty per cent, the museum would bring in $292,000 from this line of business. This would not however be the only source of revenue for the museum, now converted to a hotel museum; revenue would also be derived from food and drink, preferably served in a vintage coach.

In due course the museum could use its increased revenue to leverage financing for the construction of a world class theme-based hotel, thereby freeing the vintage coaches for tours once again by Zambians and visitors alike.

With the internet, advertising the new facility would be extremely easy, especially if the main strategy employed was targeting railway clubs around the world, all of whom have active websites.

Revamping the Livingstone Railway Museum would increase choices and provide inexpensive accommodation for both local and foreign tourists. It would also provide opportunities for local entrepreneurs who would be involved in the rehabilitation of the vintage coaches, construction of the new facilities, and supply of food and drink.

Opportunities to involve the community in this way are in fact abundant in Zambia. Some of these opportunities like the development of the Shiwa Ng'andu estate in northern Zambia are obvious and have already been successfully exploited. Others are less obvious but no less potentially lucrative.

Many Zambians are aware of the writer Wilbur Smith but few seem to realise that the famed author whose works have been translated into 26 languages, is a fellow national. Wilbur Addison Smith was born on January 9, 1933 in the central mining town of Kabwe. Although Smith has not lived in Zambia for many years he has never forgotten his heritage as evidenced by the fact that most of his writings involve the history of his homeland and Southern Africa.

Wilbur Smith has a huge international following that would be interested in visiting the land of his birth. The house Smith was born in should be turned into a heritage building accessible to his the many fans from around the world. As far as possible it should be restored to its original condition. The aim of the entrepreneur who eventually operates this venture should be to attract at least two per cent of the international Wilbur Smith fan club (estimated at more than one million) to visit the house. That would bring a minimum of 20,000 foreign tourists to Kabwe, in addition to local tourists. Even if there were no admission charge to the museum, the house would still generate significant revenue from an on-the-premises café, Wilbur Smith books, and memorabilia.

Assuming the tourists spent $10, on average, the business would generate $200,000 from foreign visitors alone, per annum. There would also be additional revenue from local tourists.

The benefits of restoring Wilbur Smith's house into a heritage home open to tourists would go beyond the income earned by the entrepreneur and the employment offered to helpers at the home. Guest houses and hotels in Kabwe would also benefit as tourists would need somewhere to sleep, as would other existing or potential tourist sites that the Smith visitors may wish to include in their itineraries.

There are many other opportunities to be exploited in this way. Certainly Chishimba Falls, Kalambo Falls, and Nkundalila Falls can all be developed with priority given to construction of low cost but comfortable accommodation attractive to local tourists. Concentrating at first on inexpensive accommodation would level the playing field and encourage the participation of Zambian entrepreneurs in the development of these spectacular sights.

Chishimba Falls, comprising the main falls, Kaela Rapids, and Mutumuna Falls, potentially has a very large market for tourists, given its closeness to Tanzania and the Tanzania Zambia railway corridor. Kalambo Falls is just as close and for a short distance the Kalambo River marks the boundary between Zambia and Tanzania.

Kalambo is second only to South Africa's Tugela Falls as the highest uninterrupted falls on the continent. But Kalambo is not just a tourist site, it is also important archaeologically. Carbon dating of tools excavated from Kalambo Gorge suggests human activity there stretching back more than 300,000 years.

For both sight-seeing and archeological reasons, Kalambo is a national treasure whose potential must be exploited urgently.

Nkundalila is also an obvious site for development. Thanks to its central Zambian location, it does get some visitors from the Copperbelt and Lusaka provinces. These visitors tend to be campers and in the absence of facilities spend little or no money in the community.

All three sites and indeed all potential tourist areas in Zambia have a huge international market to tap into.

Two examples illustrate the point. According to Statistics Canada, Canadians spent a record $3.2 billion on foreign travel between June and September 2010. That comes to $12.8 billion on an annualised basis, an increase of 5.2 per cent from a year earlier. The second example is from China.

The China Outbound Tourism Report 2009-2010 by the China Tourism Academy estimates 54 million Chinese nationals travelling abroad and spending $6.86 billion.

Zambia has good relations with both countries and could realistically mount a 'visit Zambia campaign' directed at the two countries' travelling public. It would not be unrealistic to aim for 10 per cent of tourists from these countries to include Zambia in their travel plans. Success would result in Zambia earning $1.2 billion from Canada and $686 million from China.

Unlocking Cash for investment

There are other resources available for Zambian development in addition to the potential revenue from tourism. Zambia has assets that can be liquidated and still continue to perform for the nation.

A good example comes from the health sector. Over the past thirty years, it has been fashionable for ailing Zambian political leaders to be sent abroad for treatment. Since the end of apartheid, the favourite destination for Zambia's sick politicians has been South Africa. But whether the political elite have travelled to Europe or Southern Africa for treatment, the cost to Zambia of medical-related travel has been excessive. The common excuse advanced for not using Zambian hospitals and health centres is that these institutions are not sufficiently equipped and may not have all the necessary facilities, although they may have excellent doctors.

The money spent on medical-related travel could be saved by establishing a world class hospital in Lusaka that would serve both local and international patients. The current University Teaching Hospital could be sold to an international medical group with a commitment to provision of excellent medical care. It is difficult to suggest a value for the hospital but we can be sure that its location and the solid although neglected structures would be attractive to many investors.

When the Congolese-born American basketball player, December Mutombo, paid $3m toward the cost of a feasibility study assessing the viability of building a new hospital in his homeland, the conclusion was that a 300-bed hospital could be built for $44m. That estimate was made in 1999.

The University Teaching Hospital has approximately 1655 beds and 250 baby cots. It has five times more beds than the Moomba hospital, in addition to the baby cots. On the basis of comparative capacity, the UTH should be worth $220 million. Furthermore the University Teaching Hospital has the following departments:

- Department of Anaesthesia
- Department of Internal Medicine
- Department of Obstetrics and Gynaecology
- Department of Paediatrics

- Department of Surgery
- Department of Community Medicine
- Department of Pathology
- Radiology Department
- Physiotherapy Department
- Pharmacy Department
- Blood Bank

The existence of these departments and inflation over the past decade would suggest that the UTH has a value well in excess of $220 million.

Let's be conservative however and assume a sale value of $200 million. If UTH were sold on this basis, the proceeds of sale could then be earmarked for construction of two health centres with in patient capacity in each province.

The reader will recall the Cameron Sinclair method of constructing fully equipped clinics at a cost of $200,000. The figure includes the cost of operating the facility for a year. The analysis here uses the higher figure of $400,000 per health centre because of the requirement of in patient capacity, assumed at 100.

Bearing this in mind, the $200 million realised from the sale of the University Teaching Hospital would be enough to construct two new health centres in each one of Zambia's nine provinces, create a trust fund for procurement of medicines and equipment not provided for in the national budget, and contribute to investment in the education of doctors, nurses, and other medical personnel. The proposed split would be $7.2 million; $92.8 million; and $100 million.

The new owners of the University Teaching Hospital would be obliged, as part of transition arrangements, to care for the poor pending completion of the new health centres.

In late December 2010 Yakub Mulla, the Dean of the School of Medicine at the University of Zambia lamented the absence of basic scientists, blaming the lack of progress in building more medical schools. He was however hopeful that Zambia would produce enough basic scientists to meet demand with the help of two grants received from the United States and the University of Colombia. In his words:

> The American government introduced an initiative called the Medical Education Partnership Initiative for Southern Africa worth US$130 million. Our school is among the 11 countries that have been

> selected. Zambia will receive US$2 million per year for 5 years. At the same time, the UNZA School of Medicine is among schools in three countries in Africa that have been selected under the Nursing Education Partnership Initiative of the University of Colombia to help improve the standards of nurses in the country. So we are lucky that we are recipients of two grants.

As shown above, Professor Mulla's school could get much more than the $2 million a year for five years that the Americans have promised.

Unlocking cash tied up in the UTH would allow Zambia a world class hospital able to provide medical attention previously only available abroad; build 18 new medical facilities (collectively with more beds than the UTH) mostly in rural areas; create a trust fund to help guarantee availability of medicines and vital equipment in the new hospitals; and increase investment in the education and training of medical personnel. All this would be done without resort to the disgraceful practice of begging.

In the same manner, additional resources could be unlocked for education. For example, the two Kabulonga schools (Gilbert Rennie and Jean Rennie to older readers) could be offered for sale to purchasers keen on establishing first rate secondary schools for boys and girls in Zambia. With the cost of public school education in the United Kingdom becoming prohibitive, there is huge interest in alternative ways of providing this kind of education less expensively. The two Kabulonga schools have ample premises and are located in a prime area of Lusaka and despite neglect over the past forty years they have much to offer by way of solid structures, playing fields, a swimming pool, and squash court that can be rehabilitated. Indeed the two schools were run along the lines of English boarding schools until the late 1960s.

It is not necessary for our purposes to determine the precise cash value of the two schools but we can estimate what the schools are likely to fetch. During the debate on academy schools in the United Kingdom in 2006, the British government said some non-academy schools offering a lower quality of education, cost up to £35m or US $54 million.

The cost of the average academy school on the other hand was between £25-30m or between US$ 38.7- 46.4 million. This type of academy school would be built for about 1,300 pupils.

To be competitive and encourage the right buyers, the Kabulonga schools would have to be seen as offering more than an equivalent school in England or indeed South Africa, the other destination for seekers of a relatively inexpensive English public school education.

None of the academy schools discussed has the expansive grounds and potential of the Kabulonga schools.

The potential of the two schools suggests that they could each easily fetch the going price for academy schools in England. But let's assume that each of the two schools fetched only half of the average cost of an academy school in England, the sale proceeds for both would come to $42.55 million. It is proposed that this money should be used for equipping existing schools, given the very large number of schools that are not able to function for want of basic equipment such as desks, which can be made at home.

A few years ago I visited a Zambian owned information technology college in Ndola. I was impressed by the orderliness of the establishment and could not help noticing that the college had neat functional desks finished in vinyl. I asked the owner of the college where he had got them from. Had they been imported? I still recall the smile on his face when he triumphantly explained that the desks had been made in the backyard of the premises he operated from, mostly from discarded wood. He did admit that the vinyl itself was imported.

Part of the $42.55 million raised from the sale of the two Kabulonga schools could be used to support a tender for the construction and installation of desks in schools across the country. To maximise local content and reduce costs, the vinyl could be dispensed with on this occasion!

The cost of constructing desks in North America ranges from as little as $5 to $100. Desks made in highly automated factories will have a lower unit price than desks made largely by hand.

Given lower labour costs in Zambia, desks made by hand in the country would be much cheaper than desks made by hand in North America. Assuming each Zambian district required 1000 desks at a cost of $50 per desk, the total amount payable to the suppliers of desks would be $3.65 million. Most of this money would go to individual desk manufacturers in rural or semi-urban areas, because there are more of these areas than in urban centres. The recipients of this cash would probably be peasant farmers in their other lives, and would almost certainly use part of this income to enhance their farming.

All this would be done inexpensively with the cost of making desks barely making a dent in the sale price of the Kabulonga schools, as there would still be $38.9 million left over for the creation of a trust fund to guarantee future equipment purchases and training of teachers not provided for in the national budget.

Cash in hand for people

The principle of liquidating underperforming assets in a way that enhances national development is not confined to schools and hospitals. While discussing Kanyama Township's vulnerability to flooding, mention was made of the fact that a Zambian controlled firm of property developers in South Africa did offer to convert Kanyama into a well serviced residential area with proper drainage.

Perhaps an even better candidate for this upgrading would be Kalingalinga settlement which is located in a prime area of Lusaka between the Kabulonga residential area and the Great East Road leading to the international airport. Given its location and the exceptionally high demand for good residential property in Lusaka, it would not be difficult to lease the entire settlement to property developers.

The end result of the development would be the creation of a modern residential area with proper sewage and drainage systems and recreational facilities. In order to achieve this dream a number of existing structures would of course have to be erased. These structures do however have a value to the current occupants.

The agreement allowing property developers to acquire Kalingalinga would therefore have to include provision for payment of fair compensation to people losing their homes. With this compensation the previously cash strapped residents of Kalingalinga would have more choices; they could use the money to settle farther away from urban Lusaka and invest in agriculture, or they could find other accommodation in Lusaka, or indeed invest in one of the development corporations now owning the township.

A good model for taking over Kalingalinga would be one that encouraged residents to acquire shares in the development company.

Some residents would of course choose to be bought out but others may be interested in owning shares with a real market value. The opportunity to buy shares in the new company should be open both to those deciding to stay in the new Kalingalinga as well as those deciding to leave. Encouraging this kind of ownership would also release hundreds of millions of Kwacha believed to be in mattresses in settlements like Kalingalinga, into the formal sector.

A suitable environment for growth

The policies proposed in this book are likely to lead to robust economic growth and empowerment of ordinary Zambians. Because of the increased economic activity and consequent rise in demands for virtually all products, the new Zambian economy could compound environmental challenges such as deforestation. Whether or not we blame government policy for deforestation or take the view that poverty or the poor are to blame, it is undeniable that harvesting of trees for charcoal production is a main cause of forest loss. It is therefore important that in implementing growth-oriented policies such as the ones espoused here, the government encourages the use of appropriate technology and effectively discourages deforestation.

Too many Zambians rely on charcoal for basic energy and this demand leads to destruction of trees at an unsustainable rate. It need not be that way. Zambians can get alternative energy for household purposes such as cooking that is less damaging to the environment. There is for example a solar cooker that can be built easily and cheaply and adopted as the main source of energy for households currently reliant on charcoal.

The cooker is made primarily from windscreen shade, and according to SolarCooking.org has been tested successfully around the world. The other pieces of equipment needed to make the cooker are a grill, black pot, bucket and a plastic bag. Individuals who have tried to make the cooker at home in North America have been able to do so for $10. As long as the cooker is pointed toward the sun it can get very hot, reaching a temperature of 350 degrees!

This cooker is more efficient than the traditional Zambian brazier. Serious consideration should be given to encouraging this as the main source of energy in homes currently using the brazier.

At the same time as solar energy is encouraged as a way of reducing dependency on charcoal, Zambia should seriously turn its attention to reforestation. Reforestation is crucial in the effort to improve the quality of Zambian life, as the forests soak up pollution and dust from the air, rebuild natural habitats and ecosystems, and reduce the negative impact of global warming.

There is another advantage of reforestation for Zambia - it creates an opportunity for large scale employment as thousands of people would be required to cover deforested areas across the country with new trees.

It's about the people

Zambians must be recognised as a people with the ingenuity to move their economy forward. Real economic development and prosperity can only come from Zambians, regardless of ethnicity, first language, gender, skin colour or birth circumstance. With the kinds of policies advocated in this book, Zambians do not need coercion to advance their country. They only need reaffirmation of their freedom and integrity to tap into their legendary creativity for the good of their country. Thus far the free market system so bravely reintroduced in the early 1990s has been used largely for the benefit of foreigners and Zambians chosen (or at least tolerated) for success by the regime. The commitment to merit has not been evident, and consequently innovative Zambians unknown to the political elite have been denied the opportunity to use their innovation for the good of the country.

It is time to allow an economy for the people to emerge, as only when ordinary people feel connected to the formal economy and believe in the institutions of government, will large scale employment be possible.

Government's primary role in creating the new Zambia is to institute the necessary policy framework and commit to serving their nationals without discrimination. The Zambian people will do the rest.

Epilogue

EPILOGUE

From the International Bugle-Post Newspaper

January 27, 2031

Zambia the Possible

By the Staff of Inclusive Quality World

At the end of each year we compile a list of countries that in our view offer the best quality of life to citizens. We produce an annual Index made up of ten categories, namely: Cost of Living, Culture and Leisure, Global awareness, Economy, Environment, Freedom, Public Health Care, Infrastructure, Safety and Risk, and Climate. Inevitably this involves a lot of statistical analysis from a number of sources, including government websites, civil society organisations, the World Bank, the World Health Organization, and respected journals such as *The New African*, to name but a few. We also take into account what our researchers from around the world say about congeniality of life in the countries they are based in.

This year we shall depart from tradition and not comment on each one of the top ten countries. Instead we shall concentrate on the Southern African republic of Zambia which has been voted the best country to live in for the year 2031.

The choice of Zambia will surprise many in what used to be called the 'developed world'. The surprise is understandable as barely twenty years ago Zambia was considered one of the worst managed countries in the world dependent on foreign aid even for the provision of the most basic social services. At the same time the country had avaricious elites that drove the price of things like housing beyond the reach of ordinary citizens.

The change appears to have started in early 2012 when the relatively new Freedom government encouraged the private sector to modernize shanty towns through development corporations that offered shares to residents. The effect of modernizing the previously illegal settlements was to increase the supply of suitable housing for Zambia's middle class. This in turn led to a significant drop in the cost of housing and property rentals. At the same time, there was a huge increase in real estate activity with the average real estate company in Lusaka, the Zambian capital, increasing the size of its workforce by 10 per cent.

About two years later, the country was to see an even larger growth in employment as the Zambian government's policy of only buying goods and services from within the country, bore fruit with the automotive industry alone creating 30,000 jobs between 2013 and 2014.

By 2016 there were 1.4 million people employed in the formal sector of the economy compared to 700,000 in 2008. This growth in the middle class led to unprecedented spending on culture and leisure which in turn led to reductions in the cost of local holidays, as tourist operators could now count on increased volume, rather than high prices, for their profit. Philanthropy too increased as middle class Zambians took a greater interest in the education of their children as well as the country as a whole. It is telling that all tourist sites, including the Livingstone Railway museum operated by Zambians have a library where visitors are offered educational virtual global tours. The Livingstone Railway museum also offers a biannual scholarship to a student studying locomotive engineering at any Commonwealth university.

But Zambia's critics argue that the economy is overheating and the current growth rate of 10 per cent may stoke inflation. It is certainly the case that producers of certain goods like furniture can barely meet demand. On the other hand housing prices at the close of 2030 were in relative terms lower than 2008 prices. Furthermore there has been a huge increase in food production over the past five years resulting in a real drop in prices for most foods over the past five years, partly resulting from increased investment by former shanty town dwellers that got the opportunity to unlock the cash in their dwellings and invest in small scale farming.

And commercial famers too have increased production of food for domestic consumption in response to the expanding Zambian middle class. Other factors responsible for doubling Zambian land under cultivation include improved roads and access to excellent health care for farmers, as well as availability of first rate schools for farmers' children. A survey of new immigrants conducted in June 2030 identified health care and education as the two top reasons why immigrants chose Zambia over other countries. The third reason was physical security. Zambia has recently been ranked the world's fourth safest country.

While Zambia's performance is recognised by all as impressive for a country with its history of mismanagement, there are still concerns about some of the decisions that the government takes. In 2028 for example, the ministry of science and technology endorsed a proposal that would have seen the Mongu based Mukuka Nkoloso Space Centre launch a weather monitoring satellite. The project was only abandoned after the Chinsali based Nalumino Mundia Institute for Public Policy published a highly rated paper showing the cost ineffectiveness of the project and its wastefulness given that a number of satellites that Zambia can tap into for this purpose already exist. The space centre is now encouraged to collaborate with other organisations and minimise capital expenditure.

It is possible that the Zambian economy may at some point begin to overheat. It is even possible that the government may make decisions reminiscent of earlier less democratic governments. A third challenge is one that many countries would love to have - Zambia is heading for a shortage of labour. The most recent statistics show that the number of Zambians employed in the formal sector has tripled since 2016 and now stands at 4.2 million.

Whatever happens in the future, Zambia is the story of the third decade of the century. It has shown the most remarkable improvement in the recorded history of the world. We have no hesitation in naming it the best country to live in, in 2031.

Index

L

M

N

O

CPSIA information can be obtained at www.ICGtesting.com
Printed in the USA
LVOW01s0523270515

439872LV00014BA/202/P

9 781906 704865